Rick S

POCKET

PARIS

Rick Steves, Steve Smith & Gene Openshaw

Contents

Introduction

Paris—the City of Light—has been a beacon of culture for centuries. As a world capital of art, fashion, food, literature, and ideas, it stands as a symbol of all the fine things human civilization can offer. Come prepared to celebrate this, rather than judge our cultural differences, and you'll capture the romance and joie de vivre that this city exudes.

Paris offers sweeping boulevards, farmers markets, and world-class art galleries. Sip *un café crème* with intellectuals at a sidewalk café, then step into an Impressionist painting in a tree-lined park. Visit *Mona Lisa* and *Venus de Milo* at the Louvre, and marvel at Monet and Renoir at the Orsay. Cruise the Seine, zip to the top of the Eiffel Tower, and saunter down Avenue des Champs-Elysées. Save some after-dark energy for one of the world's most romantic cities.

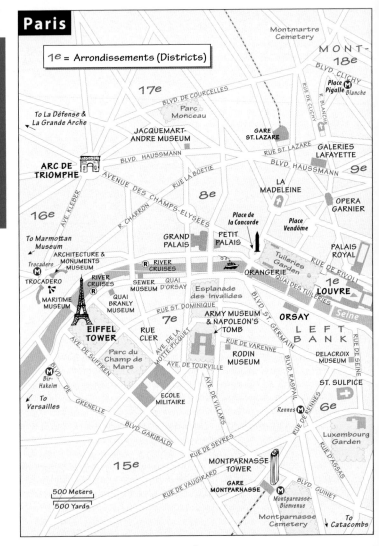

Paris

1e = Arrondissements (Districts)

Montmartre Cemetery

MONT-
18e
BLVD. CLICHY
Place
Pigalle Blanche

17e

BLVD. DE COURCELLES

To La Défense &
La Grande Arche

Parc
Monceau

JACQUEMART-
ANDRE MUSEUM

GARE
ST. LAZARE

RUE ST. LAZARE

GALERIES
LAFAYETTE

BLVD. HAUSSMANN

BLVD. HAUSSMANN

9e

ARC DE
TRIOMPHE

RUE LA BOETIE

LA
MADELEINE

OPERA
GARNIER

16e

AVENUE DES CHAMPS-ELYSEES

8e

Place de
la Concorde

Place
Vendôme

AVE. KLEBER

R. CHARRON

PALAIS
ROYAL

To Marmottan
Museum

ARCHITECTURE &
MONUMENTS
MUSEUM

Trocadero

TROCADERO

RIVER
CRUISES

GRAND
PALAIS

PETIT
PALAIS

Tuileries
Garden

RUE DE RIVOLI

1e

ORANGERIE

QUAI DES TUILERIES

LOUVRE

MARITIME
MUSEUM

RIVER
CRUISES

SEWER
MUSEUM

QUAI
D'ORSAY

Esplanade
des Invalides

Seine

QUAI
BRANLY
MUSEUM

RUE ST. DOMINIQUE

ORSAY

LEFT
BANK

EIFFEL
TOWER

RUE
CLER

7e

ARMY MUSEUM
& NAPOLEON'S
TOMB

BLVD. ST. GERMAIN

DELACROIX
MUSEUM

RUE DE VARENNE

RODIN
MUSEUM

RUE DE SEINE

AVE. DE LA
MOTTE-PICQUET

Parc du
Champ de
Mars

BLVD. RASPAIL

ST. SULPICE

Bir-
Hakeim

AVE. DE SUFFREN

AVE. DE TOURVILLE

To Versailles

AVE. DE VILLARS

ECOLE
MILITAIRE

6e

Rennes

RUE DE RENNES

Luxembourg
Garden

RUE D'ASSAS

BLVD. DE GRENELLE

BLVD. GARIBALDI

RUE DE SEVRES

15e

MONTPARNASSE
TOWER

BLVD. GUINET

RUE DE VAUGIRARD

GARE
MONTPARNASSE

Montparnasse-
Bienvenue

To
Catacombs

500 Meters
500 Yards

Montparnasse
Cemetery

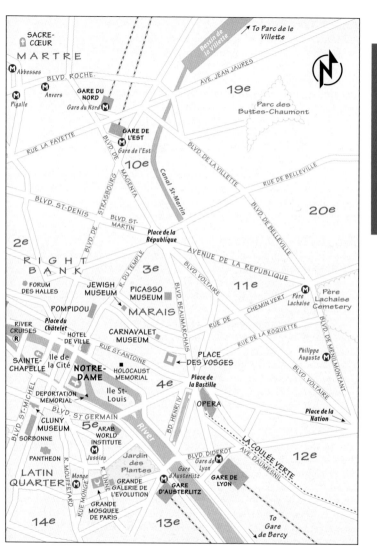

About This Book

Rick Steves Pocket Paris is a personal tour guide...in your pocket. The core of the book is six self-guided tours that zero in on Paris' greatest sights and neighborhoods. The Historic Paris Walk takes you through the heart of the city—soaring Notre-Dame, the bustling Latin Quarter, and the stained-glass wonder of Sainte-Chapelle. You'll see all the essentials of the vast Louvre and Orsay museums, while still leaving time for browsing. Ascend the 1,000-foot Eiffel Tower at sunset and watch the City of Light light up. Stroll Rue Cler's friendly shops, and take a side trip to Versailles for chandeliered palaces and manicured gardens.

The rest of this book is a traveler's tool kit, with my best advice on how to save money, plan your time, ride public transportation, and avoid lines at the busiest sights. You'll also get recommendations on hotels, restaurants, and activities.

Paris by Neighborhood

Central Paris (population 2.3 million) is circled by a ring road and split in half by the Seine River, which runs east-west. North of the Seine is the Right Bank (Rive Droite), and to the south is the Left Bank (Rive Gauche). The bull's-eye is Notre-Dame, the heart of Paris, on an island in the middle of the Seine.

Twenty arrondissements (administrative districts) spiral out from the center like an escargot shell. If your hotel's zip code is 75007, you know (from the last two digits) that it's in the 7th arrondissement. The city is peppered with Métro stops, and most Parisians locate addresses by the closest stop. So, in Parisian jargon, the Eiffel Tower is on *la Rive Gauche* (the Left Bank) in the *7ème* (7th arrondissement), zip code 75007, Mo: Trocadéro (the nearest Métro stop).

Think of Paris as a series of neighborhoods cradling major landmarks.

Historic Core: This area centers on the Ile de la Cité ("Island of the City"), located in the middle of the Seine. Here you'll find Paris' oldest sights, from Roman ruins to the medieval Notre-Dame and Sainte-Chapelle churches. Other sights in this area: Conciergerie, Archaeological Crypt, Deportation Memorial, riverside promenade and Paris Plages, and the lovely island of Ile St. Louis. Paris' most historic riverside vendors, *les bouquinistes,* line both sides of the Seine as it passes Ile de la Cité.

Paris Neighborhoods

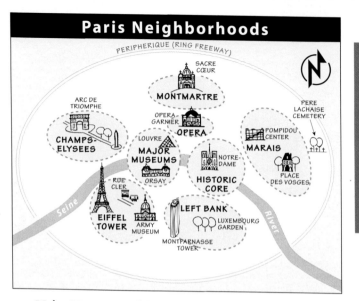

Major Museums Neighborhood: Located just west of the historic core, this is where you'll find the Louvre, Orsay, and Orangerie. Other sights are the Tuileries Garden and Palais Royal courtyards.

Champs-Elysées: The greatest of the many grand 19th-century boulevards on the Right Bank, the Champs-Elysées runs northwest from Place de la Concorde to the Arc de Triomphe. Sights in this area include the Petit and Grand Palais, Hôtel Hyatt Regency Paris Etoile (for its great city view), and La Défense with La Grande Arche.

Eiffel Tower Neighborhood: Dominated by the Eiffel Tower, this area also boasts the colorful Rue Cler (with recommended hotels and restaurants), Army Museum and Napoleon's Tomb, and Rodin Museum. Other sights are the Paris Sewer Museum and the Marmottan Museum.

Opéra Neighborhood: Surrounding the Opéra Garnier, this classy area on the Right Bank is home to a series of impressive boulevards and sights. Along with elegant sights such as the Opéra Garnier, Jacquemart-André Museum, and Fragonard Perfume Museum, the

Paris at a Glance

▲▲▲**Notre-Dame Cathedral** Paris' most beloved church is closed indefinitely. See page 149.

▲▲▲**Sainte-Chapelle** Gothic cathedral with peerless stained glass. **Hours:** Daily 9:00-19:00, Oct-March until 17:00. See page 150.

▲▲▲**Louvre** Europe's oldest and greatest museum, starring *Mona Lisa* and *Venus de Milo*. **Hours:** Wed-Mon 9:00-18:00, closed Tue. See page 151.

▲▲▲**Orsay Museum** Nineteenth-century art, including Europe's greatest Impressionist collection. **Hours:** Tue-Sun 9:30-18:00, Thu until 21:45, closed Mon. See page 151.

▲▲▲**Eiffel Tower** Paris' soaring exclamation point. **Hours:** Daily mid-June-Aug 9:00-24:45, Sept-mid-June 9:30-23:45. See page 153.

▲▲▲**Champs-Elysées** Paris' grand boulevard. See page 162.

▲▲▲**Versailles** The ultimate royal palace (Château), with a Hall of Mirrors, vast gardens, a grand canal, plus a queen's playground. **Hours:** Château Tue-Sun 9:00-18:30, Nov-March until 17:30; Trianon/Domaine Tue-Sun 12:00-18:30, Nov-March until 17:30; gardens generally daily 8:00-20:30, Nov-March until 18:00; entire complex (except the Gardens) closed Mon year-round. See page 173.

▲▲**Riverside Promenades and Paris Plages** Traffic-free riverside areas for recreation and strolling; in summer, "beaches" add more fun. **Hours:** Promenades—always strollable; Plages—mid-July-mid-Aug 8:00-24:00. See page 151.

▲▲**Orangerie Museum** Monet's water lilies and modernist classics in a lovely setting. **Hours:** Wed-Mon 9:00-18:00, closed Tue. See page 151.

▲▲**Rue Cler** Ultimate Parisian market street. **Hours:** Stores open Tue-Sat 8:30-13:00 & 15:00-19:30, Sun 8:30-12:00, dead on Sun afternoon and all day Mon. See page 156.

▲▲**Army Museum and Napoleon's Tomb** The emperor's imposing tomb, flanked by museums of France's wars. **Hours:** Daily 10:00-18:00; Napoleon's Tomb open until 21:00 on Tue. See page 156.

▲▲**Rodin Museum** Works by the greatest sculptor since Michelangelo, with many statues in a peaceful garden. **Hours:** Tue-Sun 10:00-18:30, closed Mon. See page 156.

▲▲**Marmottan Museum** Art museum focusing on Monet. **Hours:** Tue-Sun 10:00-18:00, Thu until 21:00, closed Mon. See page 157.

▲▲**Cluny Museum** Medieval art with unicorn tapestries. **Hours:** Tue-Sun 9:30-18:15, first and third Thu of the month until 21:00, closed Mon. See page 159.

▲▲**Arc de Triomphe** Triumphal arch marking start of Champs-Elysées. **Hours:** Interior daily 10:00-23:00, Oct-March until 22:30. See page 163.

▲▲**Opéra Garnier** Grand belle époque theater with a modern ceiling by Chagall. **Hours:** Generally daily 10:00-16:15, mid-July-Aug until 17:15. See page 165.

▲▲**Jacquemart-André Museum** Art-strewn 19th-century mansion. **Hours:** Daily 10:00-18:00, Mon until 20:30 during special exhibits. See page 166.

▲▲**Pompidou Center** Modern art in colorful building with city views. **Hours:** Permanent collection open Wed-Mon 11:00-21:00, closed Tue. See page 169.

▲▲**Père Lachaise Cemetery** Final home of Paris' illustrious dead. **Hours:** Mon-Fri 8:00-18:00, Sat from 8:30, Sun from 9:00, closes at 17:30 in winter. See page 170.

▲▲**Montmartre and Sacré-Cœur** Bohemian, hill-top neighborhood capped with a stunning white basilica and spectacular views. **Hours:** Daily 6:30-22:30; dome climb daily 10:00-20:00, Oct-May until 18:00, Jan-Feb until 17:00. See page 172.

▲▲**Carnavalet Museum** Paris' history wrapped up in a 16th-century mansion. **Hours:** Tue-Sun 10:00-18:00, closed Mon. See page 168.

▲**Picasso Museum** Rotating Picasso exhibits filling a three-floor mansion. **Hours:** Tue-Fri 10:30-18:00, Sat-Sun from 9:30, closed Mon. See page 169.

▲**Panthéon** Neoclassical monument/burial place of the famous. **Hours:** Daily 10:00-18:30, Oct-March until 18:00. See page 161.

neighborhood also offers high-end shopping: at Galeries Lafayette department store and around Place de la Madeleine and Place Vendôme.

Left Bank: The Left Bank is home to...the Left Bank. Anchored by the large Luxembourg Garden (near recommended hotels and eateries), the Left Bank is the traditional neighborhood of Paris' intellectual, artistic, and café life. Other sights: the Latin Quarter, Cluny Museum, St. Germain-des-Prés and St. Sulpice churches, Panthéon, Montparnasse Tower, and Catacombs. This is also one of Paris' best shopping areas.

Marais: Stretching eastward from the Pompidou Center to the Bastille along Rue de Rivoli/Rue St. Antoine, this neighborhood has recommended restaurants and hotels, shops, the delightful Place des Vosges, and artistic sights (Pompidou Center, Picasso Museum). The area is known for its avant-garde boutiques and residents. Other Marais sights: Jewish Art and History Museum, Père Lachaise Cemetery, Carnavalet Museum, and Victor Hugo's House.

Montmartre: This hill, topped by the bulbous white domes of Sacré-Cœur Basilica, hovers on the northern fringes of your Paris map. Home to recommended hotels and restaurants, Montmartre retains some of the charm that once drew Impressionist painters and turn-of-the-century bohemians. Other sights are the Montmartre Museum, Moulin Rouge, and Pigalle.

Planning Your Time

The following day plans give an idea of how much an organized, motivated, and caffeinated person can see. Trying to do too much would drive you in-Seine, so leave a few things for your next visit. Paris is a great one-week getaway. If you have less than a week, pick and choose from the sample days below.

Day 1: Follow my Historic Paris Walk, featuring Notre-Dame, the Latin Quarter, and Sainte-Chapelle. After a break in the Luxembourg Garden, visit the Cluny Museum, then tour the Opéra Garnier. Take an evening boat cruise on the Seine

Day 2: Tour the Louvre in the morning. Stroll the Champs-Elysées from the Arc de Triomphe to the Tuileries Garden, and possibly take in the Orangerie Museum. Enjoy dinner on Ile St. Louis, then a floodlit walk by Notre-Dame.

Day 3: Start the day by touring the Orsay and Rodin museums. After lunch, visit the Army Museum and Napoleon's Tomb, then take

my Rue Cler neighborhood walk and relax at a café. Finish with a stroll along the Left Bank riverside promenade. In the evening, take a bus, taxi, or retro car tour.

Day 4: Take RER/Train-C to Versailles and tour the palace's interior, followed by lunch in the Gardens and the rest of the palace sights. Return to Paris for dinner.

Day 5: Concentrate on the Marais neighborhood and tour the Carnavalet. Have lunch on Place des Vosges or Rue des Rosiers. Choose from these Marais sights: Pompidou Center, Jewish Art and History Museum, Picasso Museum, or Père Lachaise Cemetery. Enjoy a twilight ride up the Eiffel Tower and the Place du Trocadéro scene nearby.

Day 6: Take a day trip to Giverny or Chartres, or explore the shopping districts of Paris. Take in the evening scene on the Champs-Elysées and hike to the top of the Arc de Triomphe.

Day 7: There's still plenty to do: bus #69 tour followed by Père Lachaise Cemetery, Montmartre and Sacré-Cœur, Jacquemart-André Museum, Marmottan Museum, or more shopping and cafés.

When to Go

Late spring and fall bring the best weather and the biggest crowds. May, June, September, and October are the toughest months for hotel-hunting—don't expect many deals. Summers are generally hot and dry; if you wilt in the heat, look for a room with air-conditioning. Rooms are easy to land in August (some hotels offer deals), and though many French businesses close in August, you'll hardly notice.

Paris makes a great winter getaway. Airfare costs less, cafés are cozy, and the city feels lively but not touristy. Expect cold (even

Rick's Free Video Clips and Audio Tours

Rick Steves Classroom Europe, a powerful tool for teachers, is also useful for travelers. This video library contains about 500 short clips excerpted from my public television series. Enjoy these videos as you sort through options for your trip and to better understand what you'll see in Europe. Check it out at Classroom.RickSteves.com (just enter a topic to find everything I've filmed on a subject).

    Rick Steves Audio Europe, a free app, makes it easy to download my audio tours and listen to them offline as you travel. For this book (look for the 🎧), these audio tours include my Historic Paris Walk and Rue Cler Walk, and tours of the Louvre, Orsay, and Versailles. The app also offers interviews (organized by country) from my public radio show with experts from Europe and around the globe. Find it in your app store or at Rick-Steves.com/AudioEurope.

freezing lows) and rain (hats, gloves, scarves, umbrellas, and thick-soled shoes are essential).

Before You Go

You'll have a smoother trip if you tackle a few things ahead of time. For more details on these topics, see the Practicalities chapter and RickSteves.com, which has helpful travel-tip articles and videos.

    Make sure your travel documents are valid. If your passport is due to expire within six months of your ticketed date of return, you need to renew it. Allow six weeks or more to renew or get a passport (www.travel.state.gov). Check for current Covid entry requirements, such as proof of vaccination or a negative Covid-19 test result.

    Arrange your transportation. Book your international flights. Figure out your transportation options. If traveling beyond Paris, research train reservations, rail passes, and car rentals.

    Book rooms well in advance, especially if your trip falls during peak season or any major holidays or festivals.

    Reserve ahead for key sights. At some sights (the Louvre,

Sainte-Chapelle, Orangerie, and Versailles), advance reservations are required. Advance reservations are also smart for the Eiffel Tower, Catacombs, and Conciergerie.

Buy a **Paris Museum Pass** if the pass makes sense for your trip (do the math). Buy it online in advance, then use it to reserve timed-entry slots for covered sights.

Consider travel insurance. Compare the cost of insurance to the cost of your potential loss. Check whether your existing insurance (health, homeowners, or renters) covers you and your possessions overseas.

Call your bank. Alert your bank that you'll be using your debit and credit cards in Europe. Ask about transaction fees, and, if you don't already have one, get a "contactless" credit card (request your card PIN too). You don't need to bring euros; you can withdraw euros from cash machines in Europe.

Use your smartphone smartly. Sign up for an international service plan to reduce your costs, or rely on Wi-Fi in Europe instead. Download any apps you'll want on the road, such as maps, translators, transit schedules, and Rick Steves Audio Europe (see sidebar).

Pack light. You'll walk with your luggage more than you think.

I travel for weeks with a single carry-on bag and a day pack. Use the packing checklist in Practicalities as a guide.

Travel Smart

If you have a positive attitude, equip yourself with good information (this book), and expect to travel smart, you will.

Pickpockets abound in crowded places where tourists congregate. Treat commotions as smokescreens for theft. Keep your cash, credit cards, and passport secure in a money belt tucked under your clothes; carry only a day's spending money in your front pocket or wallet.

If you wilt easily, choose a hotel with air-conditioning, start your day early, take a midday siesta, and resume your sightseeing later.

Be sure to schedule in slack time for picnics, laundry, people-watching, leisurely dinners, shopping, and recharging your touristic batteries. Slow down and be open to unexpected experiences and the hospitality of the French people.

Assemble the perfect riverside picnic, linger in a cozy bistro, or challenge a local to a game of *boules*. As you visit places I know and love, I'm happy you'll be meeting some of my favorite Parisians.

Happy travels! *Bon Voyage!*

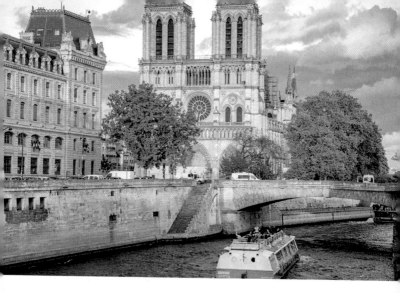

Historic Paris Walk

Ile de la Cité and the Latin Quarter

Paris has been the cultural capital of Europe for centuries. We'll start where it did, on Ile de la Cité, with a foray onto the Left Bank, on a walk that laces together 80 generations of history—from Celtic fishing village to Roman city, bustling medieval capital, birthplace of the Revolution, bohemian haunt of the 1920s café scene, and the working world of modern Paris. Along the way, we'll marvel at two of Paris' greatest sights—Notre-Dame and Sainte-Chapelle. Expect changes in the area around Notre-Dame as the cathedral undergoes reconstruction in the wake of the 2019 fire.

Allow a good four hours for this three-mile walk, including time inside the sights. Allow a little more time to pause for lunch or a *café crème,* to browse for antique books, or to watch the lazy flow of the timeless Seine.

ORIENTATION

Paris Museum Pass: Some sights on this walk are covered by the time- and money-saving Paris Museum Pass (see the Sights chapter). On Ile de la Cité, you can buy a pass at the tourist-friendly tabac/souvenir store (5 Boulevard du Palais) across the street from the Sainte-Chapelle entrance.

Notre-Dame: Due to the 2019 fire, only the cathedral's exterior is viewable. The interior and tower climb are closed for repair, and some surrounding areas may also be blocked off. For updates, see www.notredamedeparis.fr (select "Visiter"—website is in French only). Binoculars are helpful to view the church exterior (as well as Sainte-Chapelle's stained-glass windows).

Deportation Memorial: Free, daily 10:00-19:00, Oct-March until 17:00, may close at random times, free 45-minute audioguide and guided tours may be available, Mo: Cité, +33 6 14 67 54 98.

Sainte-Chapelle: €11.50 timed-entry ticket, €18.50 combo-ticket with Conciergerie, covered by Museum Pass, reserve online in advance to ensure entry (limited tickets may be available in person); daily 9:00-19:00, Oct-March until 17:00; audioguide-€3, 4 Boulevard du Palais, Mo: Cité, +33 1 53 40 60 80, www.sainte-chapelle.fr.

Expect long lines to get in. First comes the **security line** (sharp objects and glass confiscated). Next, you'll encounter the **ticket-buying line**—Museum Pass, combo, and advance-ticket holders can skip this queue.

Conciergerie: €11.50 timed-entry ticket, €18.50 combo-ticket with Sainte-Chapelle, covered by Museum Pass, book online, daily 9:30-18:00, multimedia guide-€5, 2 Boulevard du Palais, Mo: Cité, +33 1 53 40 60 80, www.paris-conciergerie.fr.

Avoiding Crowds: This area is most crowded from midmorning to midafternoon, especially on Tuesday (when the Louvre is closed) and on weekends. Generally, come early or as late in the day as possible. **Sainte-Chapelle** has limited space, and bottlenecks to get in are the norm. Its security lines are shortest first thing in the morning.

Tours: ∩ Download my free Paris Historic Walk audio tour.

THE WALK BEGINS

▶ *Start at Notre-Dame Cathedral on the island in the Seine River, the physical and historic bull's-eye of your Paris map. The closest Métro stops are Cité, Hôtel de Ville, and St. Michel.*

Notre-Dame and Nearby

Find a place where you can take in the whole scene: the church, the square (Place du Parvis), the cityscape, and visitors from around the globe. You're standing near the center of France: The small bronze plaque called "Point Zero" (embedded in the ground, 30 yards in front of the church) is the point from which all distances are measured. And you're looking at the symbolic heart of France. As you take it all in, ponder this spot's long and venerable history.

Notre-Dame through the Ages

Centuries from now, people standing here will still talk about the night of April 15, 2019, when Notre-Dame Cathedral went up in flames. That disastrous event is just one more episode in the long and fascinating story of Paris.

Think of the changes this site has seen over the years. About 2,300 years ago, there was virtually nothing here at all. This was the humble island where the Parisii tribe lived, caught fish, and sold their catch at the place where the east-west river crossed a north-south road. When the Romans conquered the Parisii, they built their Temple of Jupiter where Notre-Dame stands today (52 BC). When Rome fell, the Germanic Franks sealed their victory by replacing the temple with the Christian church of St. Etienne. Around the year 800, the Frankish

Notre-Dame—a 200-year construction project

Rose window framing "Our Lady"

Historic Paris Walk

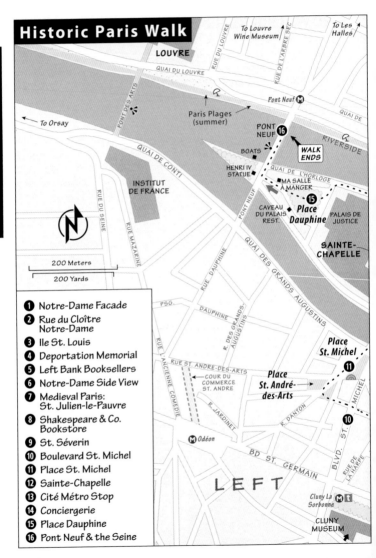

LOUVRE

To Louvre Wine Museum

To Les Halles

QUAI DU LOUVRE

RUE DU LOUVRE

RUE DE L'ARBRE SEC

Pont Neuf Ⓜ

QUAI DE

To Orsay

PONT DES ARTS

Paris Plages (summer)

PONT NEUF

16

RIVERSIDE

WALK ENDS

BOATS

QUAI DE CONTI

HENRI IV STATUE

QUAI DE L'HORLOGE

MA SALLE A MANGER

INSTITUT DE FRANCE

RUE DU SEINE

RUE MAZARINE

PONT NEUF

CAVEAU DU PALAIS REST.

15

Place Dauphine

PALAIS DE JUSTICE

N

200 Meters

200 Yards

QUAI DES GRANDS AUGUSTINS

SAINTE-CHAPELLE

RUE DAUPHINE

PSG.

DAUPHINE

R. DES GRANDS AUGUSTINS

Place St. Michel

11

MICHEL

Ⓜ **1** Notre-Dame Facade

2 Rue du Cloître Notre-Dame

3 Ile St. Louis

4 Deportation Memorial

5 Left Bank Booksellers

6 Notre-Dame Side View

7 Medieval Paris: St. Julien-le-Pauvre

8 Shakespeare & Co. Bookstore

9 St. Séverin

10 Boulevard St. Michel

11 Place St. Michel

12 Sainte-Chapelle

13 Cité Métro Stop

14 Conciergerie

15 Place Dauphine

16 Pont Neuf & the Seine

RUE ANCIENNE COMEDIE

RUE ST. ANDRE-DES-ARTS

COUR DU COMMERCE ST. ANDRE

Place St. André-des-Arts

R. JARDINET

R. DANTON

Ⓜ Odéon

BD. ST. GERMAIN

BLVD. ST.

RUE DE LA HARPE

10

LEFT

Cluny La Sorbonne Ⓜ

CLUNY MUSEUM

19

HISTORIC PARIS WALK

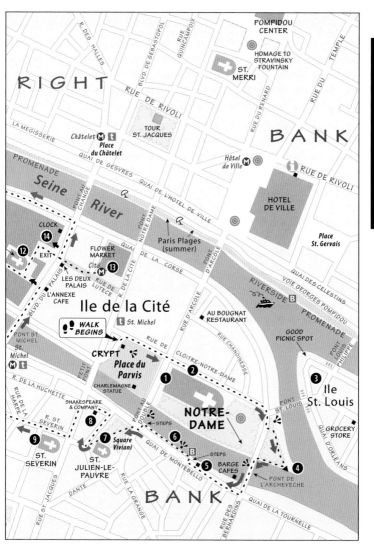

King Charlemagne (see his big equestrian statue to the right of the church) established the first glimmers of modern "France."

By the year 1200, visitors standing here would have seen (as we do today) a construction zone. The old Frankish church was being torn down and replaced with a more glorious structure renamed "Notre-Dame." Soon it was topped with a pointy spire atop the roof and two never-completed steeples in front (the two stubby bell towers we see today).

By 1800, you'd also see a crumbling church weathered by the ages and neglect. The central spire had been removed (for fear it would fall over), and there were virtually no statues on the facade (having been damaged during the Revolution). The square in front was a tangle of ramshackle medieval buildings, with Notre-Dame's bell towers rising above, inspiring Victor Hugo's story of a deformed bell-ringer who could look down on all of Paris. (The instant success of that book helped rally public interest in saving the building.)

In 1844, a 30-year-old architect named Eugène-Emmanuel Viollet-le-Duc began a massive renovation in the Neo-Gothic style. He put a new 300-foot spire atop the roof (echoing the original), and added more statues, including the fanciful gargoyles.

After 800 years of work, Notre-Dame had become a truly glorious structure, the most famous Gothic church in the world. That was the church that stood here in 2019 when it caught fire...and Paris began writing yet another chapter in its story.

▶ *In fact, much of the history of Paris still lies buried in front of the cathedral. Some has been unearthed and put on display in the **Archaeological Crypt** (to your right; see page 149 of the Sights chapter). Now turn your attention to the church.*

Point Zero: Step on the center of France.

Charlemagne, whose "Franks" became "France"

Paris Through History

250 BC: Small fishing village of the Parisii, a Celtic tribe.

52 BC: Julius Caesar conquers the Parisii capital of Lutetia (near Paris); Romans replace it with a new capital on the Left Bank.

AD 497: Roman Paris falls to the Germanic Franks. King Clovis (482-511) converts to Christianity and makes Paris his capital.

885-886: Paris under siege by Viking Norsemen = Normans.

1163: Notre-Dame cornerstone laid.

c. 1250: Paris is a bustling commercial city with a university and new construction, such as Sainte-Chapelle and Notre-Dame.

c. 1600: King Henry IV beautifies Paris with buildings, roads, bridges, and squares.

c. 1700: Louis XIV makes Versailles his capital. Parisians grumble.

1789: Paris is the heart of France's Revolution, which condemns thousands to the guillotine.

1804: Napoleon Bonaparte crowns himself emperor in a ceremony at Notre-Dame.

c. 1860: Napoleon's nephew, Napoleon III, commissions Baron Haussmann to build Paris' wide boulevards.

1889: The centennial of the Revolution is celebrated with the Eiffel Tower. Paris enjoys the prosperity of the belle époque (beautiful age).

1920s: After the draining Great War, Paris is a cheap place to live, attracting expatriates such as Ernest Hemingway.

1940-1944: Occupied Paris spends the war years under gray skies and gray Nazi uniforms.

1981-1995: Paris modernizes: the TGV, the new Louvre Pyramid, Musée d'Orsay, La Grande Arche de la Défense, and Opéra Bastille.

2015: A series of terrorist attacks throughout the city tests Parisian resolve.

2019: Parisians are shocked to see their beloved Notre-Dame catch fire. Undaunted, they vow to rebuild. Cathedral reconstruction continues with the goal of reopening in time for the 2024 Paris Olympic Games.

❶ Notre-Dame Facade

Despite the 2019 fire, the main body of the church still stands. We'll get a better look at the damaged parts later, but for now, focus on the still-breathtaking facade.

Find the circular window in the center of the facade, which frames a statue of a woman holding a baby. This church is dedicated to "Our Lady" (Notre Dame), and there she is, cradling God, right in the heart of the facade, surrounded by the halo of the rose window. Though the church is massive and imposing, it has always stood for the grace and compassion of Mary, the "mother of God."

▶ *Looking two-thirds of the way up Notre-Dame's left tower, you might spot Paris' most photographed gargoyle. Now, approach closer to the cathedral (as best you can with the construction barriers) to view the statues adorning the church's left portal.*

St. Denis: Flanking the left doorway is a man with a misplaced head—that's St. Denis, the city's first bishop and patron saint. Denis proved so successful at winning converts that the Romans' pagan priests beheaded him as a warning to those forsaking the Roman gods. But those early Christians were hard to keep down. Denis simply got up, tucked his head under his arm, headed north, paused at a fountain to wash it off, and continued until he found just the right place to meet his maker. Christianity gained ground, and a church soon replaced the pagan temple.

▶ *Now, get as close as you can to the central doorway. Over the door are scenes from the Last Judgment.*

Central Portal: It's the end of the world, and Christ sits on the throne of judgment (just under the arches, holding both hands up).

St. Denis with head in hands

Last Judgment (over the central door)

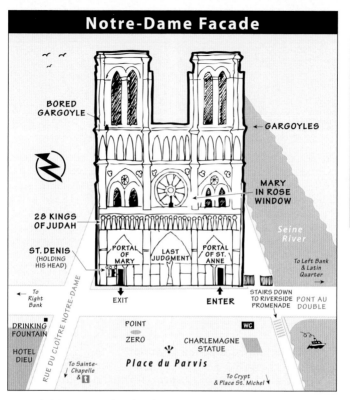

Notre-Dame Facade

BORED GARGOYLE

GARGOYLES

MARY IN ROSE WINDOW

28 KINGS OF JUDAH

ST. DENIS (HOLDING HIS HEAD)

PORTAL OF MARY

LAST JUDGMENT

PORTAL OF ST. ANNE

Seine River

To Left Bank & Latin Quarter

RUE DU CLOÎTRE NOTRE-DAME

← To Right Bank

EXIT

ENTER

STAIRS DOWN TO RIVERSIDE PROMENADE

PONT AU DOUBLE

DRINKING FOUNTAIN

HOTEL DIEU

POINT ZERO

WC

CHARLEMAGNE STATUE

Place du Parvis

To Sainte-Chapelle &

To Crypt & Place St. Michel

Beneath him an angel and a demon weigh souls in the balance; the demon cheats by pressing down. It's a sculptural depiction of the good, the bad, and the ugly. The good souls stand to the left, gazing up to heaven. The bad souls to the right are chained up and led off to a six-hour tour of the Louvre on a hot summer day.

▶ *Now look higher. Above the doorway arches is a row of 28 statues, known as...*

The Kings of Judah: In the days of the French Revolution (1789-1799), these biblical kings were mistaken for the hated French kings, and Notre-Dame represented the oppressive Catholic hierarchy. The

Notre-Dame's soaring Gothic arches

Joan of Arc—former heretic, now saint

citizens stormed the church, crying, "Off with their heads!" Plop—they lopped off the crowned heads of these kings with glee, creating a row of St. Denises that weren't repaired for decades. But the story doesn't end there. A schoolteacher collected the heads and buried them in his backyard for safekeeping. There they slept until 1977, when they were accidentally unearthed. Today, you can stare into the eyes of the original kings in the **Cluny Museum,** a few blocks away (see the Sights chapter).

▶ *Remember that Notre-Dame is more than a tourist sight—it's been a place of worship for nearly a thousand years. Close your eyes and imagine the church in all its glory. Since the interior is currently closed to visitors, let's remove our metaphorical hats and mentally "step inside" the church, to take a...*

Virtual Tour of Notre-Dame's Interior

"Enter" the church like a simple bareheaded peasant of old (referring to the modern "Notre-Dame Interior" map). Imagine stepping into a dark, earthly cavern lit with an unearthly light from the stained-glass windows. The priest intones the words of the Mass that echo through the hall. Your eyes follow the slender columns up 10 stories to the praying-hands arches of the ceiling. Walk up the long central **nave** lined with columns and flanked by side aisles. The place is huge—it can hold up to 10,000 faithful for a service.

When you reach the altar, you're at the center of this cross-shaped church, where the faithful receive the bread and wine of Communion. This was the holy spot for Romans, Christians...and even atheists. When the Revolutionaries stormed the church, they gutted it and

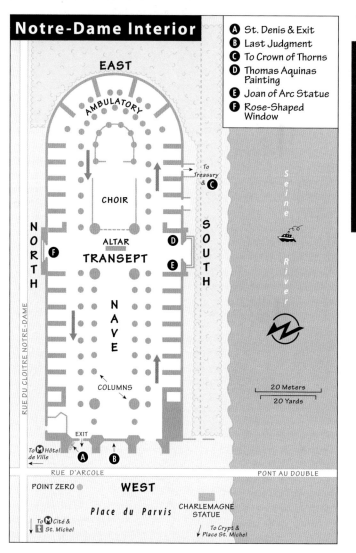

Notre-Dame Interior

- **A** St. Denis & Exit
- **B** Last Judgment
- **C** To Crown of Thorns
- **D** Thomas Aquinas Painting
- **E** Joan of Arc Statue
- **F** Rose-Shaped Window

EAST

AMBULATORY

CHOIR

To Treasury & **C**

NORTH

F

ALTAR

TRANSEPT

D

E

SOUTH

Seine River

N A V E

COLUMNS

RUE DU CLOITRE NOTRE-DAME

20 Meters

20 Yards

EXIT

To **M** Hôtel de Ville

A

B

RUE D'ARCOLE

PONT AU DOUBLE

POINT ZERO

WEST

Place du Parvis

CHARLEMAGNE STATUE

To **M** Cité & **T** St. Michel

To Crypt & Place St. Michel

Original rose window in north transept

A scene depicting the resurrection of Jesus

turned it into a "Temple of Reason," complete with a woman dressed like Lady Liberty holding court at the altar.

If you were able to browse around the church, you'd see it's become a kind of Smithsonian for **artifacts** near and dear to the heart of the Parisian people. There's the venerated Crown of Thorns that supposedly Jesus wore (kept safely in the Treasury). There's the gilded-and-enameled reliquary dedicated to St. Geneviève (fifth century), whose prayers saved Paris from Attila the Hun. A painting honors the scholar Thomas Aquinas (1225-1274), who studied at the University of Paris while writing his landmark theological works fusing faith and reason. There's a statue of Joan of Arc, the teenager who rallied her country to drive English invaders from Paris. (Though she was executed, the former "witch" was later beatified—right here in Notre-Dame.)

The oldest feature inside the church is the blue-and-purple rose-shaped window in the north transept—still with its original medieval glass, though not viewable. A new feature is the huge white tarp covering the roof above to prevent rain from entering the church during reconstruction. Finish your virtual visit by pausing at one of the many chapels. Here the faithful can pause in your mental tour to meditate and light a (virtual) candle in hopes that someday soon the interior will be restored to its former glory.

▶ *Let's circle around the left (north) side of the church, walking down the street called...*

❷ Rue du Cloître Notre-Dame

As you head toward the back of the church, you'll pass fascinating information panels describing (in English) the fire and its aftermath, the recovered rooster from the steeple's top, and the restoration process.

You'll also get your most up-close-and-personal view of the building. Notice gaps where stained-glass windows were removed—each panel is being tested for lead to ensure they're safe for restoration work to begin. Get close to a flying buttress, now supported by wooden structures.

▶ *Keep going past the church. (Don't worry, we'll get another classic look at Notre-Dame later, from just across the river.) After passing the garden behind the cathedral, pause for a moment on the arched pedestrian-only bridge, Pont St. Louis, for a look at...*

❸ Ile St. Louis

If Ile de la Cité is a tugboat laden with the history of Paris, it's towing this classy little residential dinghy, laden only with high-rent apartments, boutiques, characteristic restaurants, and famous ice cream shops. Consider taking a brief detour across the pedestrian bridge, Pont St. Louis, to explore this little island (or come back in the evening).

▶ *Let's head toward the Left Bank. Start walking south (with the backside of Notre-Dame on your right). Enter the little grassy park to your left, where (behind a tall green hedge) you'll find the...*

❹ Deportation Memorial
(Mémorial de la Déportation)

This memorial to the 200,000 French victims of the Nazi concentration camps (1940-1945) draws you into their experience. France was quickly overrun by Nazi Germany, and Paris spent the war years under Nazi occupation. Jews and dissidents were rounded up and deported—many never returned.

As you descend the steps, the city around you disappears. Surrounded by walls, you have become a prisoner. Inside, the hallway is lined with 200,000 lighted crystals, one for each French citizen who died. Flickering at the far end is the eternal flame of hope. Above the exit as you leave is the message you'll find at many other Holocaust sites: "Forgive, but never forget."

▶ *Return to ground level. Exit the garden, turn left, and cross the bridge (Pont de l'Archevêché). When you reach the Left Bank, turn right along the river and work your way along the south side of Notre-Dame. We're now turning our attention to the neighborhood around us, the...*

Deportation Memorial's 200,000 points of light | Booksellers line the Seine River.

Left Bank

❺ Left Bank Booksellers

The Rive Gauche, or the Left Bank of the Seine—"left" if you were floating downstream—still has many of the twisting lanes and narrow buildings of medieval times. The Right Bank near the Seine is more modern and business-oriented, with wide boulevards and stressed Parisians in suits.

Here along the riverbank, the "big business" is secondhand books, displayed in the green metal stalls on the parapet (called *bouquinistes*). These literary entrepreneurs pride themselves on their easygoing style. With flexible hours and virtually no overhead, they run their businesses as they have since the mid-1500s.

▸ *At a gap in the green stalls directly across from Notre-Dame, find stairs leading down to the river—good for losing crowds and for a terrific...*

❻ Notre-Dame Side View

From this side, you can really appreciate both the church architecture and the devastation wrought by the 2019 fire. Before the fire, you'd have seen a green lead-covered roof topped with Viollet-le-Duc's 300-foot steeple, and several statues adorning its base.

Those are gone completely, as is the lead roof and all windows—save for the three massive rose windows (now covered for protection). But what's surprising is how much of the church survived. That's a testament to the medieval architects who designed this amazing structure. Their great technological innovation is what we've come to call the **Gothic style.**

In a glance, you can spot many of the elements of Gothic:

pointed arches, the lacy stone tracery of the windows, pinnacles, statues on rooftops, and pointed steeples covered with the prickly "flames" (Flamboyant Gothic) of the Holy Spirit. Most distinctive of all are the **flying buttresses.** These 50-foot stone "beams" that stick out of the church were the key to the complex Gothic architecture. The pointed arches built inside the church cause the weight of the roof to push outward rather than downward. The "flying" buttresses support the roof by pushing back inward. Gothic architects were masters at playing architectural forces against each other to build loftier and loftier churches, opening the walls for stained-glass windows. The Gothic style was born here in Paris. Those wooden structures you see supporting the flying buttresses show how they were originally raised.

Picture Quasimodo (the fictional hunchback) limping around the roof among the "gargoyles." These grotesque beasts sticking out from pillars and buttresses represent souls caught between heaven and earth. They also function as rainspouts (from the same French root word as "gargle") when there are no evil spirits to battle.

▶ *Continue walking along the river. When you reach the bridge (Pont au Double) at the front of Notre-Dame, head back up the stairs, veer left across the street, and find a small park called Square Viviani. Angle across the square and pass by Paris' oldest inhabitant—an acacia tree nicknamed Robinier, after the guy who planted it in 1602. Imagine that this same tree might once have shaded the Sun King, Louis XIV. Just beyond the tree you'll find the small rough-stone church of St. Julien-le-Pauvre. Leave the park, walking past the church, to tiny Rue Galande.*

It takes 13 tourists to build a Gothic church: one steeple, six columns, and six buttresses.

❼ Medieval Paris

Picture Paris in 1250, when the **church of St. Julien-le-Pauvre** was still new. You can pop into the church for a trip east a few hundred miles and back a few centuries. Back outside, continue around the church a few steps. Notre-Dame was nearly built, Sainte-Chapelle had just opened, the university was expanding human knowledge, and Paris was fast becoming a prosperous industrial and commercial center. The area around the church and along Rue Galande gives you some of the medieval feel of ramshackle architecture and old houses leaning every which way. In medieval days, people were piled on top of each other, building at all angles, as they scrambled for this prime real estate near the main commercial artery of the day—the Seine. The smell of fish competed with the smell of neighbors in this knot of humanity.

▶ *Return toward the river and turn left on Rue de la Bûcherie to find...*

❽ Shakespeare and Company Bookstore

In addition to hosting butchers and fishmongers, the Left Bank has been home to scholars, philosophers, and poets since medieval times. This funky bookstore—a reincarnation of the original shop from the 1920s on Rue de l'Odéon—has picked up the literary torch. Sylvia Beach, an American with a passion for free thinking, opened Shakespeare and Company for the post-WWI Lost Generation, who came to Paris to find themselves. American writers flocked to the city for the cheap rent, fleeing the uptight, Prohibition-era United States. Beach's bookstore was famous as a meeting place for the likes of Ernest Hemingway, James Joyce, Gertrude Stein, and Ezra Pound.

▶ *Continue to Rue du Petit-Pont and turn left. This bustling north-south boulevard (which becomes Rue St. Jacques) was the Romans' busiest*

St. Julien-le-Pauvre and 400-year-old tree

This bookstore carries on expatriate bohemian life.

St. Séverin flickers with flamboyant flames.   The Latin Quarter looks "Greek" today.

street 2,000 years ago, with chariots racing in and out of the city.
Turn right at the Gothic church of St. Séverin and walk into the Latin
Quarter.

❾ St. Séverin and the Latin Quarter

Don't ask me why, but building St. Séverin church took a century longer than building Notre-Dame. This is Flamboyant, or "flame-like,"
Gothic, and you can see how the short, prickly spires are meant to
make this building flicker in the eyes of the faithful. The church gives
us a close-up look at gargoyles, the decorative drain spouts that also
functioned to keep evil spirits away.

   Although it may look more like the Greek Quarter today (cheap
gyros abound), this area is the Latin Quarter, named for the language
you'd have heard on these streets if you walked them in the Middle
Ages. The University of Paris (founded 1215), one of the leading educa-
tional institutions of medieval Europe, was (and still is) nearby.

   Walking along Rue St. Séverin, note how the street slopes into
a central channel of bricks. In the days before plumbing and toilets,
when people still went to the river or neighborhood wells for their water, flushing meant throwing it out the window. At certain times of
day, maids on the fourth floor would holler, *"Garde de l'eau!"* ("Watch
out for the water!") and heave it into the streets, where it would eventually wash down into the Seine. Until the 19th century, all of Paris
was like this—a medieval tangle of small streets. The international feel
of this area is nothing new—it's been a melting pot and university district for almost 800 years.

▶ *At the fork with Rue de la Harpe, bear slightly right to continue down*
  Rue St. Séverin another block until you come to...

Eateries Along This Walk

The following spots make for a nice lunch or snack break (see the "Historic Paris Walk" map at the beginning of this chapter):

Ile St. Louis: Stop for gelato at Berthillon or Amorino Gelati; for crêpes and a view visit the recommended Café Med.

Ile de la Cité: L'Annexe Café offers reasonably priced café fare. For a full meal, consider Les Deux Palais, across from Sainte-Chapelle's exit, or Au Bougnat, near Notre-Dame (26 Rue Chanoinesse).

Place Dauphine: Food refuges on this dreamy square include the expensive Caveau du Palais and the funky Ma Salle à Manger.

Barges in the Seine: Docked near Notre-Dame are barges, some housing cafés with stunning views.

Place St. André-des-Arts: Two nice outdoor restaurants sit amid the bustle on this tree-filled square near Place St. Michel.

⑩ Boulevard St. Michel

Busy Boulevard St. Michel (or "boul' Miche") is famous as the main artery for Paris' café and arts scene, culminating a block away (to the left) at the intersection with Boulevard St. Germain. Although nowadays you're more likely to find leggings at 30 percent off, there are still many cafés, boutiques, and bohemian haunts nearby.

The Sorbonne—the University of Paris' humanities department—is also nearby, if you want to make a detour, though visitors are not allowed to enter. (Turn left on Boulevard St. Michel and walk two blocks south.) Originally founded as a theological school, the Sorbonne expanded to include other subjects. Nonconformity is a tradition here, and Paris remains a world center for new intellectual trends.

▶ *Cross Boulevard St. Michel. Just ahead is a tiny tree-filled square called* **Place St. André-des-Arts.** *Adjoining this square toward the river is the triangular Place St. Michel, with a Métro stop and a statue of St. Michael killing a devil.*

Place St. Michel, where revolutionaries gather

Sainte-Chapelle—built for the Crown of Thorns

⓫ Place St. Michel

You're standing at the traditional core of the Left Bank's artsy, liberal, hippie, bohemian district of poets, philosophers, winos, and *baba cools* (neo-hippies). Nearby, you'll find international eateries, far-out bookshops, street singers, pale girls in black berets, jazz clubs, and—these days—tourists.

In less commercial times, Place St. Michel was a gathering point for the city's malcontents and misfits. In 1830, 1848, and again in 1871, the citizens took the streets from the government troops, set up barricades *Les Miz*-style, and fought against royalist oppression. During World War II, the locals rose up against their Nazi oppressors (read the plaques under the dragons at the foot of the St. Michel fountain). In the spring of 1968, a time of social upheaval all over the world, young students battled riot batons and tear gas by digging up the cobblestones on the street and hurling them at police. They took over the square and declared it an independent state.

Demonstrations still take place here but the cobblestones have been replaced with pavement, so future scholars can never again use the streets as weapons.

▶ *Head toward the prickly steeple of Sainte-Chapelle. Cross the river on Pont St. Michel and continue north along the Boulevard du Palais until you reach the doorway (on your left).*

⓬ Sainte-Chapelle

Security is strict at the Sainte-Chapelle complex because this is more than a tourist attraction: France's Supreme Court meets to the right of Sainte-Chapelle in the Palais de Justice. You'll need a timed-entry ticket to go inside, and the church entry may be hidden behind a line

Sainte-Chapelle

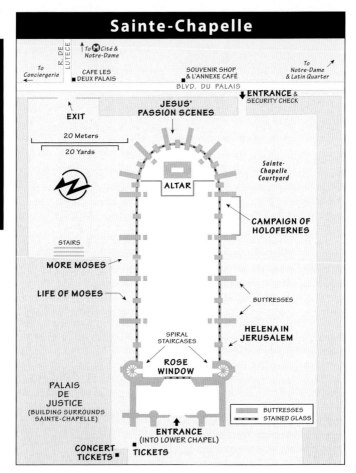

↑ To Ⓜ Cité &
Notre-Dame

R. DE LUTECE

To
Concergerie

CAFE LES
DEUX PALAIS ■

SOUVENIR SHOP
& L'ANNEXE CAFÉ

BLVD. DU PALAIS

To
Notre-Dame
& Latin Quarter

↓ ENTRANCE &
SECURITY CHECK

EXIT

JESUS'
PASSION SCENES

Sainte-
Chapelle
Courtyard

20 Meters

20 Yards

ALTAR

CAMPAIGN OF
HOLOFERNES

STAIRS

MORE MOSES

LIFE OF MOSES

BUTTRESSES

HELENA IN
JERUSALEM

SPIRAL
STAIRCASES

ROSE
WINDOW

PALAIS
DE
JUSTICE
(BUILDING SURROUNDS
SAINTE-CHAPELLE)

BUTTRESSES
STAINED GLASS

ENTRANCE
(INTO LOWER CHAPEL)

CONCERT
TICKETS ■

■ TICKETS

of ticket buyers. Once past security, you'll enter the courtyard outside Sainte-Chapelle, where you'll find information about upcoming church concerts.

This triumph of Gothic church architecture is a cathedral of glass like no other. It was speedily built between 1242 and 1248 for King

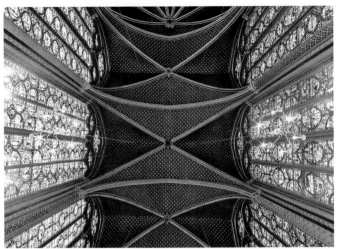

Sainte-Chapelle's crisscross arches and slim columns make the walls of stained glass possible.

Louis IX—the only French king who is now a saint—to house the supposed Crown of Thorns (later moved to Notre-Dame's treasury and now in safekeeping since the fire). Its architectural harmony is due to the fact that it was completed under the direction of one architect and in only six years—unheard of in Gothic times. Recall that Notre-Dame took more than 200 years.

Though the inside is beautiful, the exterior is basically functional. The muscular buttresses hold up the stone roof, so the walls are essentially there to display stained glass. The lacy spire is Neo-Gothic—added in the 19th century.

▶ *Climb the spiral staircase to the Chapelle Haute. Leave the rough stone of the earth and step into the light.*

Stained Glass

Fiat lux. "Let there be light." From the first page of the Bible, it's clear: Light is divine. Light shines through stained glass like God's grace shining down to earth. Gothic architects used their new technology to turn dark stone buildings into lanterns of light. The glory of Gothic shines brighter here than in any other church.

Stained Glass Supreme

Artisans made glass—which is, essentially, melted sand—using this recipe:

- Melt one part sand with two parts wood ash.
- Mix in rusty metals to get different colors—iron makes red; cobalt makes blue; copper, green; manganese, purple; cadmium, yellow.
- Blow glass into a cylinder shape, cut lengthwise, and lay flat to cool.
- Cut into pieces with an iron tool, or by heating and cooling a select spot to make it crack.
- Fit pieces together to form a figure, using strips of lead to hold them in place.
- Place masterpiece so high on a wall that no one can read it.

There are 15 separate panels of stained glass (6,500 square feet—two-thirds of it 13th-century original), with more than 1,100 different scenes, mostly from the Bible. These cover the entire Christian history of the world, from the Creation in Genesis (first window on the left, as you face the altar), to the coming of Christ (over the altar), to the end of the world (the round "rose"-shaped window at the rear of the church). Each individual scene is interesting, and the whole effect is overwhelming. Allow yourself a few minutes to bask in the glow of the colored light before tackling the individual window descriptions below.

▶ *Working clockwise from the entrance, look for these notable scenes. (The sun lights up different windows at various times of day. Overcast days give the most even light. On bright, sunny days, some sections are glorious, while others look like sheets of lead.) The first window on the left (with scenes from Genesis) is always dark because of a building butted up against it. Let's pass over that one and turn to the second window on the left.*

Life of Moses (second window, dark bottom row of diamond panels): The first panel shows baby Moses in a basket, placed by his sister in the squiggly brown river. Next he's found by the pharaoh's daughter. Then he grows up. And finally, he's a man, a prince of Egypt on his royal throne.

Jesus' Passion Scenes (directly over the altar and behind the canopy): These scenes from Jesus' arrest and Crucifixion were the backdrop for this chapel's *raison d'être*—the Crown of Thorns, which was originally displayed on this altar. Stand close to the steps of the altar—about five paces away—and gaze through the canopy where, if you look just above the altar table, you'll see Jesus, tied to a green column, being whipped. To the immediate right is the key scene in this relic chapel—Jesus (in purple robe) being fitted with the painful Crown of Thorns.

Campaign of Holofernes (window to the right of the altar wall): On the bottom row, focus on the second circle from the left. It's a battle scene (the campaign of Holofernes) showing three soldiers with swords slaughtering three men. Examine the details. The background is blue. The men have different-colored clothes—red, blue, green, mauve, and white. You can actually see the folds in the robes, the hair, and facial features. Look at the victim in the center—his head is splotched with blood. Details like these were created either by scratching on the glass or by baking on paint. It was a painstaking process of finding just the right colors, fitting them together to make a scene...and then multiplying by 1,100.

Rose Window (above entrance): It's Judgment Day, with a tiny Christ in the center, presiding over a glorious moment of wonders and miracles.

Altar

The altar was raised up high to better display the Crown of Thorns, the relic around which this chapel was built. Notice the staircase:

Campaign of Holofernes, one detail of many

Altar for the Crown of Thorns

Access was limited to the priest and the king, who wore the keys to the shrine around his neck.

King Louis IX, convinced he'd found the real McCoy, spent roughly the equivalent of €500 million for the Crown, €370 million for the gem-studded shrine to display it in (later destroyed in the French Revolution), and a mere €150 million to build Sainte-Chapelle to house it.

Lay your camera on the ground and shoot the ceiling. Those pure and simple ribs growing out of the slender columns are the essence of Gothic structure.

▶ *Exit Sainte-Chapelle. Back outside, walk counterclockwise around the church to reach the street. You'll pass by the giant* **Palais de Justice,** *the home of the French Supreme Court. The motto* Liberté, Egalité, Fraternité *over the doors is a reminder that this was also the headquarters of the Revolutionary government. Here they doled out justice, condemning many to imprisonment in the Conciergerie downstairs—or to the guillotine.*

Pass through the big iron gate to the noisy Boulevard du Palais. Cross the street to the wide, pedestrian-only Rue de Lutèce and walk about halfway down to see the ⓭ **Cité "Metropolitain" Métro Stop,** *with one of Paris's few surviving original subway entrances (early 20th century), now preserved as a national art treasure for its curvy, plantlike Art Nouveau ironwork.*

Double back to the Palais de Justice, turn right onto Boulevard du Palais, and enter the Conciergerie.

⓮ Conciergerie

Though barren inside, this former prison echoes with history. The Conciergerie was the last stop for 2,780 victims of the guillotine, including France's last *ancien régime* queen, Marie-Antoinette.

Inside, pick up a free map and breeze through the one-way, well-described circuit. See the spacious, low-ceilinged Hall of Men-at-Arms (Room 1), originally a guards' dining room. Continue to the raised area at the far end of the room (Room 4, today's bookstore). This was the walkway of the executioner, who was known affectionately as "Monsieur de Paris." Past the bookstore, find the Office of the Keeper (or "Concierge"), who admitted prisoners, monitored torture...and recommended nearby restaurants. The next cell is where condemned

The Conciergerie—a photogenic torture chamber—held prisoners awaiting the guillotine.

Original Art Nouveau Métro entrance

Marie-Antoinette's cell in the Conciergerie

prisoners combed their hair or touched up their lipstick before their final public appearance—waiting for the open-air cart (tumbrel) to pull up outside. The tumbrel would carry them to the guillotine, which was on Place de la Concorde.

Upstairs is a memorial room with the names of the 2,780 citizens condemned to death by the guillotine. While most of the famous names have been vandalized (Charlotte Corday, Robespierre, Louis XVI), you may see Marie-Antoinette (opposite the entry, 10 rows down, look for *Capet Marie-Antoinette*). Head down the hallway past more cells that give a sense of the poor and cramped conditions. Go downstairs, where—tucked behind heavy gray curtains—is a tiny chapel built on the site where Marie-Antoinette's prison cell originally stood. The chapel's three paintings tell her sad story: First, Marie stoically says goodbye to her grieving family. Next, she awaits her fate. Finally, she piously kneels in her cell to receive the Last Sacrament on the night before her beheading.

Outside in the "Cour de Femmes" courtyard, where female prisoners were allowed a little fresh air, look up and notice the spikes still guarding from above…and be glad you can leave this place with your head intact. It wasn't so easy for enemies of the state. On October 16, 1793, Marie-Antoinette stepped onto the cart, and was slowly carried to Place de la Concorde, where she had her date with "Monsieur de Paris."

▶ *Back outside, turn left on Boulevard du Palais. On the corner is the city's oldest public clock, from 1334. Turn left onto Quai de l'Horloge and walk along the river. The bridge up ahead is Pont Neuf, where we'll end this walk. At the first corner, veer left into a sleepy triangular square called…*

Pont Neuf—400-year old "new bridge"

⓯ Place Dauphine

It's amazing to find such coziness in the heart of Paris. This city of more than two million is still a city of neighborhoods, a collection of villages. The French Supreme Court building looms behind like a giant marble gavel. Enjoy the village-Paris feeling in the park. For eating recommendations on this square, see the "Eateries Along this Walk" sidebar, earlier.

▶ *Continue through Place Dauphine. As you pop out the other end, you're face-to-face with a statue of **Henry IV** (1553-1610). Though not as famous as his grandson, Louis XIV, Henry helped make Paris what it is today—a European capital of elegant buildings (the Louvre's Grand Gallery), quiet squares (Place Dauphine), and majestic bridges (Pont Neuf, to your right). Walk onto the old bridge and pause at the little nook halfway across.*

⓰ Pont Neuf and the Seine

This "new bridge" is now Paris' oldest. Built during Henry IV's reign (about 1600), its arches span the widest part of the river. Unlike other bridges, this one never had houses or buildings growing on it. The turrets were originally for vendors and street entertainers. From the bridge, look downstream (west) to see the next bridge, the pedestrian-only Pont des Arts. Ahead on the Right Bank is the long Louvre museum. Beyond that, on the Left Bank, is the Orsay. And what's that tall black tower in the distance?

Our walk ends where Paris began—on the **Seine River.** From Dijon to the English Channel, the Seine meanders 500 miles, cutting through the center of Paris. The river is shallow and slow within the city, but still dangerous enough to require steep stone embankments (built 1910) to prevent occasional floods.

In summer, the riverside *quais* are turned into beach zones with beach chairs and tanned locals, creating the Paris *Plages* (see the Sights chapter). Any time of year, you'll see tourist boats and the commercial barges that carry 20 percent of Paris' transported goods. And on the banks, locals today cast into the waters once fished by Paris' original Celtic inhabitants.

▶ *We're done. You can take a boat tour that leaves from near the base of Pont Neuf on the island side (Vedettes du Pont Neuf). The nearest Métro stop is Pont Neuf, across the bridge on the Right Bank. Bus #69 heads east along Quai du Louvre (at the north end of the bridge) and west along Rue de Rivoli (a block farther north). In fact, from here you can go anywhere—you're standing in the heart of Paris.*

Louvre Tour

Musée du Louvre

Paris' world-class museums walk you through world history, and the best place to start your "art-yssey" is at the Louvre. With more than 30,000 works of art on display, the Louvre is a full inventory of Western civilization. To cover it all in one visit is impossible. Let's focus on the Louvre's specialties—Greek sculpture, Italian painting, and French painting.

We'll see "Venuses" through history, from prehistoric stick figures to the curvy *Venus de Milo* to the wind-blown *Winged Victory of Samothrace,* and from placid medieval Madonnas to the *Mona Lisa* to the symbol of modern democracy. Each generation defined beauty differently, and we'll gain insight into long-ago civilizations by admiring what they found beautiful.

Cost: €17 timed-entry ticket required (purchase online in advance), covered by Museum Pass. Tickets include special exhibits; re-entry is not allowed (don't leave the security check area as you travel between the wings of the museum).

Hours: Wed-Mon 9:00-18:00, closed Tue; last entry 45 minutes before closing. The museum may stay open into the evening on Wed and Fri.

Information: +33 1 40 20 53 17, recorded info +33 1 40 20 51 51, www. louvre.fr.

Reserved Entry Time Required: All visitors—including Museum Pass holders—must reserve a time slot. You can generally book a reservation time up to a few hours before your visit; a day or more before is better.

Buying Tickets/Passes at the Louvre: If you arrive *sans* ticket or reservation (bad idea) and are allowed in (unlikely), in very quiet times it may be possible to buy a €15 timed-entry ticket (in side room under the pyramid). The "Museum Pass Tabac" (a.k.a. La Civette du Carrousel) sells the Museum Pass for no extra charge (cash only). It's in the underground Carrousel du Louvre mall—to find it, follow *Museum Pass* signs inside the mall.

Renovations: Due to renovations, some sections are routinely closed one day a week. Other renovations affect room numbers—expect changes to the room numbers provided in this tour.

When to Go: Crowds can be miserable on Sun, Mon (the worst day), Wed, and in the morning. Evening visits (when available) are quieter.

Main pyramid entrance

The underground mall entrance is less crowded.

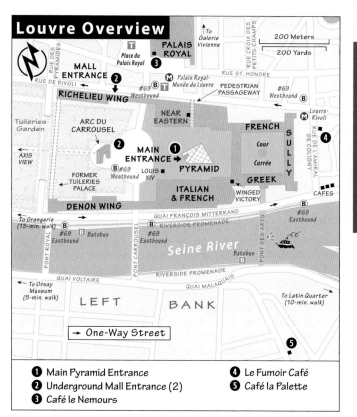

Louvre Overview

200 Meters
200 Yards

To Galerie Vivienne

PALAIS ROYAL

Place du Palais Royal ❸

RUE CROIX DES PETITS CHAMPS

RUE DE RIVOLI

RUE DES PYRAMIDES

MALL ENTRANCE ❷

RICHELIEU WING

Palais Royal-Musée du Louvre

RUE ST. HONORE

PEDESTRIAN PASSAGEWAY

#69 Westbound ⒷⓉ

#69 Westbound Ⓑ

Louvre-Rivoli Ⓜ

Tuileries Garden

ARC DU CARROUSEL

NEAR EASTERN

FRENCH

Cour Carrée

S U L L Y

RUE DE L'AMIRAL DE COLIGNY

❹

AXIS VIEW

❷ MAIN ENTRANCE ➡

Ⓑ#69 Westbound

LOUIS XIV

PYRAMID ❶

GREEK

FORMER TUILERIES PALACE

ITALIAN & FRENCH

WINGED VICTORY

CAFES

DENON WING

QUAI FRANÇOIS MITTERRAND

RIVERSIDE PROMENADE

#69 Eastbound Ⓑ

To Orangerie (15-min. walk) Ⓑ

#69 Eastbound Ⓑ Batobus

#69 Eastbound

PONT CARROUSEL

PONT ROYAL

Seine River

Batobus Ⓑ

PONT DES ARTS

QUAI VOLTAIRE

RIVERSIDE PROMENADE

QUAI MALAQUAIS

To Orsay Museum (5-min. walk)

LEFT   BANK

To Latin Quarter (10-min. walk)

➡ One-Way Street

❺

❶ Main Pyramid Entrance
❷ Underground Mall Entrance (2)
❸ Café le Nemours
❹ Le Fumoir Café
❺ Café la Palette

Getting There: Métro stop Palais Royal-Musée du Louvre is closest. Eastbound bus #69 stops along the Seine River; the best stop is labeled *Quai François Mitterrand.* Westbound #69 stops in front of the pyramid. You'll find a taxi stand on Rue de Rivoli, next to the Palais Royal-Musée du Louvre Métro station.

Getting In: There is no grander entry than through the **main entrance** at the pyramid in the central courtyard. With your timed-entry ticket, you'll scoot right in (find the line that corresponds to your ticket type). The less crowded **underground mall**

entrance is accessed through the Carrousel du Louvre shopping mall. Enter the mall at 99 Rue de Rivoli, directly from the Métro stop Palais Royal-Musée du Louvre (exit to *Musée du Louvre-Le Carrousel du Louvre*), or via the Tuileries Garden entrance close to the arch. Inside the mall, continue toward the inverted pyramid next to the Louvre's security entrance. (Don't follow signs to the *Passholders* entrance, which is a long detour away.)

Tours: English-language **guided tours** leave from inside the *Accueil des Groupes* area, under the pyramid (1.5 hours, at 11:00 and possibly at 14:00 in peak season; book in advance online, €12 plus admission, tour +33 1 40 20 52 63). **Multimedia guides** (€5) provide commentary on about 700 masterpieces.

🎧 Download my free Louvre Museum **audio tour.**

Length of This Tour: Allow at least two hours.

Baggage Check: You can store your bag in self-service lockers under the pyramid. No bags bigger than a small day bag are allowed in the galleries.

Services: WCs are located under the pyramid. Once you're in the galleries, WCs are scarce.

Cuisine Art: The Louvre has several cafés. The best is **$$ Café Mollien,** near the end of our tour (on the terrace overlooking the pyramid). A self-service **$ cafeteria** is up the escalator from the pyramid in the Richelieu wing. **$$$ Bistrot Benoit** under the pyramid is pricier. In the underground shopping mall, the **Carrousel du Louvre** has a food court upstairs with fast-food eateries. For a classy post-Louvre lunch, try **$$ Café le Nemours** (leaving the Louvre, cross Rue de Rivoli and veer left to 2 Place Colette), **$$$ Le Fumoir** (6 Rue de l'Amiral de Coligny, near Mo: Louvre-Rivoli), or **$$ Café la Palette** (15-minute walk on the other side of the river, 43 Rue de Seine).

Starring: *Venus de Milo, Winged Victory, Mona Lisa,* Leonardo da Vinci, Raphael, Michelangelo, the French painters, and many of the most iconic images of Western civilization.

THE TOUR BEGINS

▶ *Start by picking up the free map at the information desk beneath the* ***glass pyramid*** *as you enter and take a moment to orient yourself.*

Surviving the Louvre

The Louvre, the largest museum in the Western world, fills three wings of this immense, U-shaped palace. The **Richelieu wing** (north side) houses Near Eastern antiquities, decorative arts, and French, German, and Northern European art. The **Sully wing** (east side) has extensive French painting and collections of ancient Egyptian and Greek art. We'll concentrate on the Louvre's south side: the **Denon** and **Sully** wings, which hold many of the superstars, including ancient Greek sculpture, Italian Renaissance painting, and French Neoclassical and Romantic painting.

Be aware that the sprawling Louvre is constantly shuffling its deck. Rooms close, room numbers change, and pieces can be on loan or in restoration. Zero in on the biggies, and try to finish the tour with enough energy left to browse.

▶ *From the pyramid, head for the Denon wing. Ride the escalator up one floor. After showing your ticket, continue ahead 25 paces, take the first left, follow the* Antiquités Grecques *signs, and climb a set of stairs to the brick-ceilinged Salle (Room) 170: Grèce Préclassique. Enter prehistory.*

Greece (3000 BC-AD 1)

Pre-Classical Greek statues are noble but crude. In the first glass cases, find Greek Barbie dolls (3000 BC) that are older than the pyramids. These prerational voodoo dolls whittle women down to their life-giving traits. Halfway down the hall, a miniature woman (*Dame d'Auxerre*) pledges allegiance to stability. Nearby, another woman (*Core*) is essentially a column with breasts. These statues stand like they have a gun to their backs—hands at sides, facing front, with sketchy muscles and mask-like faces. "Don't move." The early Greeks, who admired statues like these, found stability more attractive than movement.

But around 450 BC, Greece entered its Golden Age, a cultural explosion that changed the course of history. Over the next 500 years, Greece produced art that was rational, orderly, and balanced. The

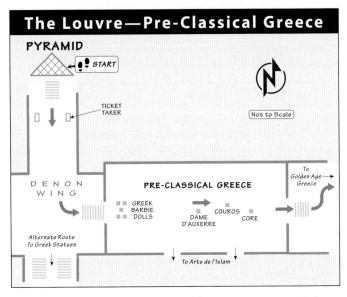

The Louvre—Pre-Classical Greece

PYRAMID

START

TICKET TAKER

Not to Scale

To Golden Age Greece →

DENON WING

PRE-CLASSICAL GREECE

GREEK BARBIE DOLLS

DAME D'AUXERRE

COUROS

CORE

Alternate Route To Greek Statues

To Arts de l'Islam

balance between timeless stability and fleeting movement made beauty. Most of the art that we'll see in the Louvre either came from or was inspired by Greece.

▶ Let's head for one of the ancient world's finest statues. Exit at the far end of the pre-Classical Greece galleries, and climb the stairs one flight. At the top, veer left (toward 11 o'clock, cross through the domed room), and continue into the Sully wing. After about 50 yards, turn right into Salle 345, where you'll find Venus de Milo floating above a sea of worshipping tourists. It's been said that among the warlike Greeks, this was the first statue to unilaterally disarm.

Venus de Milo, a.k.a. Aphrodite, late second century BC

This goddess of love created a sensation when she was discovered in 1820 on the Greek island of Melos. Europe was already in the grip of a classical fad, and this statue seemed to sum up all that ancient Greece stood for. The Greeks pictured their gods in human form (meaning

Venus de Milo—balance of opposites

Athena in the Gallery of Statues

humans are godlike), and Venus' well-proportioned body captures the balance and orderliness of the Greek universe.

Split *Venus* down the middle from nose to toes and see how the two halves balance each other. Venus rests on her right foot (a position called *contrapposto,* or "counterpoise"), then lifts her left leg, setting her whole body in motion. As the left leg rises, her right shoulder droops down. And as her knee points one way, her head turns the other, giving a balanced S-curve to her body (especially noticeable from the back).

The smooth skin of her upper half sets off the rough-cut texture of her dress (size 14). She's actually made from two different pieces of stone plugged together at the hips (the seam is visible). The face is realistic and anatomically accurate, but it's also idealized, a goddess, too generic and too perfect. This isn't any particular woman, but Everywoman—idealized features that appealed to the Greeks.

What were her missing arms doing? Some say her right arm held her dress, while her left arm was raised. Others say she was hugging a male statue or leaning on a column. I say she was picking her navel.

▶ *Orbit* Venus. *This statue is interesting and different from every angle. Remember the view from the back—we'll see it again later. Now make your reentry to earth. Follow Venus' gaze and browse around this long hall.*

Gallery of Statues

Greek statues feature the human body in all its splendor. The anatomy is accurate, and the poses are relaxed and natural. Around the fifth century BC, Greek sculptors learned to capture people in motion and to show them from different angles, not just face-forward. The classic

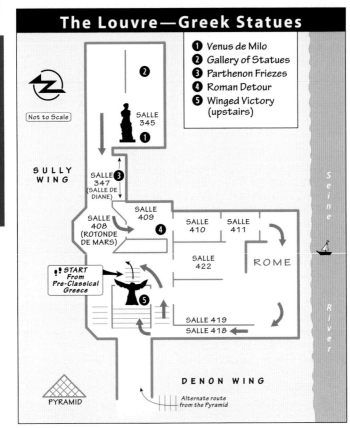

The Louvre—Greek Statues

1. Venus de Milo
2. Gallery of Statues
3. Parthenon Friezes
4. Roman Detour
5. Winged Victory (upstairs)

Not to Scale

SULLY WING

SALLE 345 — 1

SALLE 347 (SALLE DE DIANE) — 3

SALLE 408 (ROTONDE DE MARS)

SALLE 409

4

SALLE 410

SALLE 411

SALLE 422

ROME

START From Pre-Classical Greece

5

SALLE 419

SALLE 418

Seine River

DENON WING

PYRAMID

Alternate route from the Pyramid

contrapposto pose—with the weight resting on one leg—captures a balance between timeless stability and fleeting motion.

In this gallery, you'll see statues of gods, satyrs, soldiers, athletes, and everyday people engaged in ordinary activities. For Athenians, the most popular goddess was their patron, Athena. She's usually shown as a warrior, wearing a helmet and carrying a (missing) spear, ready to fight for her city. A monumental version of Athena stands at one end of the hall—the goddess of wisdom facing the goddess of love (*Venus de Milo*). Whatever the statue, Golden Age artists sought the perfect balance between down-to-earth humans (with human flaws and quirks) and the idealized perfection of Greek gods.

▶ *Head to Salle 347 (also known as Salle de Diane), located behind the Venus de Milo. (Facing Venus, find Salle 347 to your right, back the way you came.) You'll find two carved panels on opposite walls.*

Parthenon Friezes, mid-fifth century BC

These stone fragments once decorated the exterior of the greatest Athenian temple, the Parthenon, built at the peak of the Greek golden age. A model of the Parthenon shows where the panels might have hung. The centaur panel would have gone above the entrance. The panel of young women was placed under the covered colonnade, but above the doorway (to see it in the model, you'll have to crouch way down and look up).

The panel on the right side of the room shows a centaur sexually harassing a woman, as these rude creatures crashed a party of regular people. But the humans fought back and threw out their enemy. The panel was meant to represent Athens defeating its Persian invaders.

The other relief shows the sacred procession of young women who marched up the temple hill every four years with an embroidered shawl for the 40-foot-high statue of Athena, the goddess of wisdom. Carved in only a couple of inches of stone, they're amazingly realistic. They glide along horizontally (their belts and shoulders all in a line), while the folds of their dresses drape down vertically. The man in the center is relaxed, realistic, and *contrapposto*. Notice the veins in his arm. The maidens' pleated dresses make them look as stable as fluted

Parthenon frieze—natural movement

Roman busts—warts-and-all realism

columns, but their arms and legs step out naturally—their human forms emerging gracefully from the stone.

▶ *Keep backtracking another 20 paces, turning left into Salle 409, the Roman Antiquities room* (Antiquités Romaines), *for a...*

Roman Detour (Salles 409-418)

Stroll among the Caesars and try to see the person behind the public persona. Besides the many faces of the ubiquitous Emperor *Inconnu* ("unknown"), you might spot Augustus (Auguste), the first emperor, and his wily wife, Livia (Livie). Her son Tiberius (Tibère) was the Caesar that Jesus Christ "rendered unto." Caligula was notoriously depraved, curly-haired Domitia murdered her husband, Hadrian popularized the beard, Trajan ruled the Empire at its peak, and Marcus Aurelius (Marc Aurèle) presided stoically over Rome's slow fall.

The pragmatic Romans (500 BC-AD 500) were great conquerors but bad artists. One area in which they excelled was realistic portrait busts, especially of their emperors, who were worshipped as gods on earth. Fortunately for us, the Romans also had a huge appetite for Greek statues and made countless copies, adding a veneer of sophistication to their homes, temples, baths, and government buildings.

▶ *To reach the* Winged Victory *continue clockwise through the Roman collection, which eventually spills out at the base of the stairs leading up to the first floor and the dramatic...*

Winged Victory of Samothrace, 190 BC

This woman with wings, poised on the prow of a ship, once stood on an island hilltop to commemorate a naval victory. Her clothes are wind-blown and sea-sprayed, clinging to her body. Originally, her right arm was stretched high, celebrating the victory like a Super Bowl champion, waving a "we're number one" finger.

This is the *Venus de Milo* gone Hellenistic, from the time after the culture of Athens was spread around the Mediterranean by Alexander the Great (c. 325 BC). As *Victory* strides forward, the wind blows her and her wings back. Her feet are firmly on the ground, but her wings (and missing arms) stretch upward. She is a pillar of vertical strength, while the clothes curve and whip around her. These opposing forces create a feeling of great energy, making her the lightest two-ton piece of rock in captivity.

Winged Victory—wind-blown exuberance

Crown jewels in the Apollo Gallery

The earlier golden age Greeks may have considered this statue ugly. Her rippling excitement is a far cry from the dainty Parthenon maidens and the soft-focus beauty of *Venus*. And the statue's off-balance pose, like an unfinished melody, leaves you hanging. But Hellenistic Greeks loved these cliff-hanging scenes of real-life humans struggling to make their mark.

In the glass case nearby is *Victory*'s open right hand with an outstretched finger, found in 1950, a century after the statue itself was unearthed. When the French learned the hand was in Turkey, they negotiated with the Turkish government for the rights to it. Considering all the other ancient treasures that France had looted from Turkey, the Turks thought it only appropriate to give the French the finger.

▶ *Enter the octagonal room to the left as you face the* Winged Victory, *with Icarus bungee-jumping from the ceiling. Find a friendly window and look out toward the pyramid.*

The Louvre as a Palace

Formerly a royal palace, the Louvre was built in stages over eight centuries. The original medieval fortress was the part over your right shoulder (as you face the pyramid), which is today's Sully wing. Then the Tuileries Palace was built about 500 yards away, in the now-open area past the pyramid and the triumphal arch. Succeeding kings tried to connect the palaces, each monarch adding another section onto the long, skinny north and south wings. Finally, in 1852, after three centuries of building, the two palaces were connected, creating a rectangular Louvre. Nineteen years later, the Tuileries Palace burned down during a riot, leaving the U-shaped Louvre we see today.

The glass pyramid was designed by Chinese-born American

architect I. M. Pei (1989). Many Parisians initially hated the pyramid, just as they had hated another new and controversial structure 100 years earlier—the Eiffel Tower.

In the octagonal room, find the plaque at the base of the dome. The inscription reads: *"Le Musée du Louvre, fondé le 16 Septembre, 1792."* The museum was founded by France's Revolutionary National Assembly—the same people who brought you the guillotine. What could be more logical? You behead the king, inherit his palace and art collection, open the doors to the masses, and *voilà!* You have Europe's first public museum.

▶ *From the octagonal room, enter the Apollo Gallery* (Galerie d'Apollon).

Apollo Gallery

This gallery gives us a feel for the Louvre as the glorious home of French kings (before Versailles). Imagine a candlelit party in this room, drenched in stucco and gold leaf, with tapestries of leading Frenchmen and paintings featuring mythological and symbolic themes. The crystal vases, the inlaid tables, and many other art objects show the wealth of France, Europe's number-one power for two centuries. Portraits on the walls depict great French kings: Henry IV, who built the Pont Neuf; Louis XIV, the Sun King; and François I, who brought Leonardo da Vinci (and the Italian Renaissance) to France.

Stroll past glass cases of royal dinnerware to the far end of the room. In a glass case are the crown jewels. The display varies, but you may see the jewel-studded crowns of Louis XV and the less flashy Crown of Charlemagne, along with the 140-carat Regent Diamond, which once graced crowns worn by Louis XV, Louis XVI, and Napoleon.

▶ *A rare WC is a half-dozen rooms away, near Salle 650 in the Sully wing. The Italian collection* (Peintures Italiennes) *is on the other side of* Winged Victory. *Cross back in front of* Winged Victory *and enter the Denon wing and Salle 706, where you'll find two* **Botticelli frescoes** *that give us a preview of how ancient Greece would be "reborn" in the Renaissance. Now continue into the large Salle 708.*

Cimabue—2-D cardboard cutouts

Giotto—hints of 3-D and humanism

The Medieval World (1200-1500)

Cimabue, *The Madonna and Child in Majesty Surrounded by Angels*, c. 1280

During the Age of Faith (1200s), almost every church in Europe had a painting like this one. Mary was a cult figure—even bigger than the late-20th-century Madonna—adored and prayed to by the faithful for bringing Baby Jesus into the world. After the collapse of the Roman Empire (c. AD 500), medieval Europe was a poor and violent place, with the Christian Church as the only constant.

Altarpieces tended to follow the same formula: somber iconic faces, stiff poses, elegant folds in the robes, and generic angels. Cimabue's holy figures are laid flat on a gold background like cardboard cutouts, existing in a golden never-never land, as though the faithful couldn't imagine them as flesh-and-blood humans inhabiting our dark and sinful earth.

Giotto, *St. Francis of Assisi Receiving the Stigmata*, c. 1295-1300

Francis of Assisi (c. 1181-1226), a wandering Italian monk of renowned goodness, kneels on a rocky Italian hillside, pondering the pain of Christ's torture and execution. Suddenly, he looks up, startled, to see Christ himself, with six wings, hovering above. Christ shoots lasers from his wounds to the hands, feet, and side of the empathetic monk, marking him with the stigmata. Francis went on to breathe the spirit of the Renaissance into medieval Europe. His humble love of man and nature inspired artists like Giotto to portray real human beings with real emotions, living in a physical world of beauty.

Like a good filmmaker, Giotto (c. 1266-1337) doesn't just *tell* us what happened, he *shows* us in the present tense, freezing the scene at its most dramatic moment. Though the perspective is crude—Francis' hut is smaller than he is, and Christ is somehow shooting at Francis while facing us—Giotto creates the illusion of three dimensions, with a foreground (Francis), middle ground (his hut), and background (the hillside). In the predella (the panel of paintings beneath the altarpiece), birds gather at Francis' feet to hear him talk about God.

▶ *The long Grand Gallery displays Italian Renaissance painting—some masterpieces, some not.*

Italian Renaissance (1400-1600)

Built in the late 1500s to connect the old palace with the Tuileries Palace, the **Grand Gallery** displays much of the Louvre's Italian Renaissance art. From the doorway, look to the far end and consider this challenge: I hold the world record for the Grand Gallery Heel-Toe-Fun-Walk-Tourist-Slalom, going end to end in 1 minute, 58 seconds (only two injured). Time yourself. Along the way, notice some of the features of Italian Renaissance painting:

- **Religious:** Lots of Madonnas, children, martyrs, and saints.
- **Symmetrical:** The Madonnas are flanked by saints—two to the left, two to the right, and so on.
- **Realistic:** Real-life human features are especially obvious in the occasional portrait.
- **Three-Dimensional:** Every scene gets a spacious setting with a distant horizon.
- **Classical:** You'll see some Greek gods and classical nudes, but even Christian saints pose like Greek statues, and Mary is a Venus whose face and gestures embody all that was good in the Christian world.

Leonardo da Vinci, *The Virgin and Child with St. Anne*, c. 1510

Three generations—grandmother, mother, and child—are arranged in a pyramid, with Anne's face as the peak and the lamb as the lower right corner. Within this balanced structure, Leonardo sets the figures in motion. Anne's legs are pointed to our left. (Is Anne *Mona*? Hmm.) Her daughter Mary, sitting on her lap, reaches to the right. Jesus looks at her playfully while turning away. The lamb pulls away from him. But even with all the twisting and turning, this is still a

The Louvre—Grand Gallery

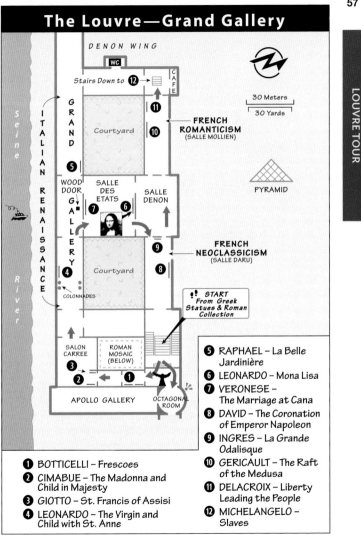

LOUVRE TOUR

DENON WING

WC

Stairs Down to ⑫ → CAFÉ

30 Meters
30 Yards

GRAND GALLERY

ITALIAN RENAISSANCE

Courtyard

FRENCH ROMANTICISM
(SALLE MOLLIEN)

⑪
⑩

PYRAMID

⑤

WOOD DOOR

SALLE DES ETATS

SALLE DENON

⑦ ⑥

FRENCH NEOCLASSICISM
(SALLE DARU)

⑨

④

Courtyard

⑧

COLONNADES

START
From Greek Statues & Roman Collection

Seine River

SALON CARREE

ROMAN MOSAIC (BELOW)

①

③
②

APOLLO GALLERY

OCTAGONAL ROOM

① BOTTICELLI – Frescoes
② CIMABUE – The Madonna and Child in Majesty
③ GIOTTO – St. Francis of Assisi
④ LEONARDO – The Virgin and Child with St. Anne

⑤ RAPHAEL – La Belle Jardinière
⑥ LEONARDO – Mona Lisa
⑦ VERONESE – The Marriage at Cana
⑧ DAVID – The Coronation of Emperor Napoleon
⑨ INGRES – La Grande Odalisque
⑩ GERICAULT – The Raft of the Medusa
⑪ DELACROIX – Liberty Leading the People
⑫ MICHELANGELO – Slaves

Leonardo's *The Virgin and Child with St. Anne*—three generations of love

placid scene. It's as orderly as the geometrically perfect universe created by the Renaissance god.

There's a psychological kidney punch in this happy painting. Jesus, the picture of childish joy, is innocently playing with a lamb—the symbol of his inevitable sacrificial death.

The Louvre has the greatest collection of Leonardos in the world—five of them. Look for the neighboring *Virgin of the Rocks* and *John the Baptist*. Leonardo was the consummate Renaissance Man; a musician, sculptor, engineer, scientist, and sometime painter, he combined knowledge from all these areas to create beauty. If he were alive today, he'd create a Unified Field Theory in physics—and set it to music.

▶ *Continue about 20 yards (past the crowded* Mona Lisa *room—where we'll head in a moment). On the right side, look for a masterpiece by Raphael.*

Raphael adopted Leonardo's trademark pyramid composition for *La Belle Jardinière*.

Italian Renaissance

A thousand years after Rome fell, plunging Europe into the Dark Ages, the Greek ideal of beauty was reborn in 15th-century Italy. The Renaissance—or "rebirth" of the culture of ancient Greece and Rome—was a cultural boom that changed people's thinking about every aspect of life. In politics, it meant democracy. In religion, it meant a move away from Church dominance and toward the assertion of man (humanism) and a more personal faith. Science and secular learning were revived after centuries of superstition and ignorance. In architecture, it was a return to the balanced columns and domes of Greece and Rome.

In painting, the Renaissance meant realism, and for the Italians, realism was spelled "3-D." Artists rediscovered the beauty of nature and the human body. With pictures of beautiful people in harmonious 3-D surroundings, they expressed the optimism and confidence of this new age.

Raphael, *La Belle Jardinière*, c. 1507

Raphael perfected the style Leonardo pioneered. This configuration of Madonna, Child, and John the Baptist is also a balanced pyramid with hazy grace and beauty. Mary is a mountain of maternal tenderness (the title translates as "The Beautiful Gardener") as she eyes her son with a knowing look and holds his hand in a gesture of union. Jesus looks up innocently, standing *contrapposto* like a chubby Greek statue. Baby John the Baptist kneels lovingly at Jesus' feet, holding a cross that hints at his playmate's sacrificial death. The interplay of gestures and gazes gives the masterpiece both intimacy and cohesiveness, while Raphael's blended brushstrokes varnish the work with an iridescent smoothness.

With Raphael, the Greek ideal of beauty—reborn in the Renaissance—reached its peak. His work spawned so many imitators who cranked out sickly sweet, generic Madonnas that we often take him for granted. Don't. This is the real thing.

▶ *The* Mona Lisa (La Joconde) *is a few steps away, in Salle 711. Mona is alone behind glass on her own false wall.(You can't miss her. Just follow the signs and the people…it's the only painting you can hear. With all the crowds, you can even smell it.)*

Leonardo's *Mona Lisa*

Veronese's Venetian party scene

Leonardo da Vinci, *Mona Lisa,* 1503-1506

When François I invited Leonardo to France, the artist—determined to pack light—brought only a few paintings with him. One was a portrait of Lisa del Giocondo, the wife of a wealthy Florentine merchant. François immediately fell in love with the painting, making it the centerpiece of the small collection of Italian masterpieces that would, in three centuries, become the Louvre museum. He called it *La Gioconda* (*La Joconde* in French)—a play on both her last name and the Italian word for "happiness." We know it as the *Mona Lisa*—a contraction of the Italian for "my lady Lisa."

Mona may disappoint you. She's smaller than you'd expect, darker, engulfed in a huge room, and hidden behind a glaring pane of glass. So, you ask, "Why all the hubbub?" Let's take a closer look. As you would with any lover, you've got to take her for who she is, not what you'd like her to be.

The famous smile attracts you first. Leonardo used a hazy technique called *sfumato,* blurring the edges of her mysterious smile. Try as you might, you can never quite see the corners of her mouth. Is she happy? Sad? Tender? Or is it a cynical supermodel's smirk? All visitors read it differently, projecting their own moods onto her enigmatic face. *Mona* is a Rorschach inkblot...so, how are you feeling?

Now look past the smile and the eyes that really do follow you (most eyes in portraits do) to some of the subtle Renaissance elements that make this painting work. The body is surprisingly massive and statue-like, a perfectly balanced pyramid turned at an angle, so we can see its mass. Her arm rests lightly on the armrest of a chair, almost on the level of the frame itself, as if she's sitting in a window looking out at us. The folds of her sleeves and her gently folded hands are remarkably realistic and relaxed. The typical Leonardo landscape shows distance by getting hazier and hazier.

Though the portrait is generally accepted as a likeness of Lisa del Giocondo, other hypotheses about the sitter's identity have been suggested, including the idea that it's Leonardo himself. Or she might be the Mama Lisa. A recent infrared scan revealed that she has a barely visible veil over her dress, which may mean (in the custom of the day) that she had just had a baby.

The overall mood is one of balance and serenity, but there's also an element of mystery. *Mona*'s smile and long-distance beauty are subtle and elusive, tempting but always just out of reach, like strands of a street singer's melody drifting through the Métro tunnel. *Mona* doesn't knock your socks off, but she winks at the patient viewer.

▸ *Before leaving* Mona, *step back and just observe the paparazzi scene. The huge canvas opposite* Mona *is...*

Paolo Veronese, *The Marriage at Cana*, 1562-1563

Stand 10 steps away from this enormous canvas to where it just fills your field of vision, and suddenly...you're in a party! Help yourself to a glass of wine. This is the Renaissance love of beautiful things gone hog-wild.

In a spacious setting of Renaissance architecture, colorful lords and ladies, decked out in their fanciest duds, feast on a great spread of food and drink, while the musicians fuel the fires of good fun. Servants prepare and serve the food, jesters play, and animals roam. In the upper left, a dog and his master look on. A sturdy linebacker in yellow pours wine out of a jug (right foreground). The man in white samples some and thinks, "Hmm, not bad," while nearby a ferocious cat battles a lion. The wedding couple at the far left is almost forgotten.

Believe it or not, this is a religious work showing the wedding celebration in which Jesus turned water into wine. And there's Jesus in the dead center of 130 frolicking figures, wondering if maybe a nonalcoholic beverage would have been a better choice. With true Renaissance optimism, Venetians pictured Christ as a party animal, someone who loved the created world as much as they did.

▸ *Exit behind* Mona *into the Salle Denon (Room 701). The dramatic Romantic room is to your left, and the grand Neoclassical room is to your*

Napoleon (center) crowns himself and his wife Josephine (kneeling) while the pope looks on.

right. After entering the Neoclassical room (Salle Daru, Room 702), kneel before the largest canvas in the Louvre.

French Painting (1780-1850)

Jacques-Louis David, *The Coronation of Emperor Napoleon*, 1806-1807

Napoleon holds aloft an imperial crown. This common-born son of immigrants is about to be crowned emperor of a "New Rome." He has just made his wife, Josephine, the empress, and she kneels at his feet. Seated behind Napoleon is the pope, who journeyed from Rome to place the imperial crown on his head. But Napoleon feels that no one is worthy of the task. At the last moment, he shrugs the pope aside, grabs the crown, holds it up for all to see...and crowns himself. The pope looks p.o.'d.

After the French people decapitated their king during the Revolution (1793), their fledgling democracy floundered in chaos. France was united by a charismatic, brilliant, temperamental, upstart general who kept his feet on the ground, his eyes on the horizon, and his hand in his coat—Napoleon Bonaparte. Napoleon quickly conquered most of Europe and insisted on being made emperor (not merely king). The painter David (dah-VEED) recorded the coronation for posterity.

The radiant woman in the gallery in the background center wasn't actually there. Napoleon's mother couldn't make it to see her boy become the most powerful man in Europe, but he had David paint her in anyway. (There's a key on the frame telling who's who in the picture.)

The coronation took place in Notre-Dame Cathedral, which was fitted with fake columns and arches to reflect the glories of Greece and the grandeur of Rome.

David was the new emperor's official painter and propagandist, in charge of color-coordinating the costumes and flags for public ceremonies and spectacles. (Find his self-portrait with curly gray hair in the *Coronation,* way up in the second balcony, peeking around the tassel directly above Napoleon's crown.) As a painter, David's clean, simple style and Greek themes championed the Neoclassical style that influenced generations of artists.

▶ *As you double back toward the Romantic room, stop at Jean-Auguste-Dominique Ingres'* **La Grande Odalisque** *(1814)—a horizontal take on* Venus de Milo's *backside. Cross back through the Salle Denon and into Room 700, gushing with French Romanticism.*

Théodore Géricault, *The Raft of the Medusa,* 1819

In the artistic war between hearts and minds, the heart style was known as Romanticism. Stressing motion and emotion, it was the flip

Ingres' *Odalisque*—cool Neoclassicism

Géricault's *Raft*—fevered Romanticism

side of cool, balanced Neoclassicism, though they both flourished in the early 1800s.

What better setting for an emotional work than a shipwreck? Clinging to a raft is a tangle of bodies and lunatics sprawled over each other. The scene writhes with agitated, ominous motion—the ripple of muscles, churning clouds, and choppy seas. On the right is a deathly green corpse dangling overboard. The face of the man at left, cradling a dead body, says it all—the despair of spending weeks stranded in the middle of nowhere.

This painting was based on an actual event—150 shipwrecked people were set adrift on the open seas for 12 days, suffering hardship and hunger, even resorting to cannibalism—only 15 survived. The story was made-to-order for a painter determined to shock the public—young Géricault (ZHAIR-ee-ko). He interviewed survivors and honed his craft, sketching dead bodies in the morgue and the twisted faces of lunatics in asylums, capturing the moment when all hope is lost.

But wait. There's a stir in the crowd. Someone has spotted something. The bodies rise up in a pyramid of hope, culminating in a flag wave. They signal frantically, trying to catch the attention of the tiny ship on the horizon, their last desperate hope...which did finally save them. If art controls your heartbeat, this is a masterpiece.

Eugène Delacroix, *Liberty Leading the People,* 1831

The year is 1830. King Charles has just issued the 19th-century equivalent of the Patriot Act, and his subjects are angry. Parisians take to the streets once again, *Les Miz*-style, to fight royalist oppressors. The people triumph—replacing the king with Louis-Philippe, who is happy to rule within the constraints of a modern constitution. There's a hard-bitten proletarian with a sword (far left), an intellectual with a top hat and a sawed-off shotgun, and even a little boy brandishing pistols.

Leading them on through the smoke and over the dead and dying is the figure of Liberty, a strong woman waving the French flag. Does this symbol of victory look familiar? It's the *Winged Victory,* wingless and topless.

To stir our emotions, Delacroix (del-ah-kwah) uses only three major colors—the red, white, and blue of the French flag. France is the symbol of modern democracy, and this painting has long stirred its citizens' passion for liberty.

This symbol of freedom is a fitting tribute to the Louvre, the first

Delacroix's *Lady Liberty*—in the classic pose of the *Winged Victory*—leads the French onward.

museum ever opened to the common rabble of humanity. The good things in life don't belong only to a small, wealthy part of society, but to everyone. The motto of France is *Liberté, Egalité, Fraternité*—liberty, equality, and brotherhood for all.

▶ *Exit the room at the far end (past the Café Mollien) and go downstairs, where you'll bump into the bum of a large, twisting male nude looking like he's just waking up after a thousand-year nap.*

Epilogue

Michelangelo, *Slaves*, 1513-1515

These two statues by the earth's greatest sculptor are an appropriate end to this museum—works that bridge the ancient and modern worlds. Michelangelo, like his fellow Renaissance artists, learned from the Greeks. The perfect anatomy, twisting poses, and idealized faces appear as if they could have been created 2,000 years earlier.

The so-called *Dying Slave* (also called the *Sleeping Slave*, looking

Michelangelo's *Slaves*

A victim of the Louvre

like he should be stretched out on a sofa) twists listlessly against his T-shirt-like bonds, revealing his smooth skin. Compare the polished detail of the rippling, bulging left arm with the sketchy details of the face and neck. With Michelangelo, the body does the talking. This is probably the most sensual nude that Michelangelo, the master of the male body, ever created.

The *Rebellious Slave* fights against his bondage. His shoulders rotate one way, his head and leg turn the other. He looks upward, straining to get free. He even seems to be trying to release himself from the rock he's made of. Michelangelo said that his purpose was to carve away the marble to reveal the figures God put inside. This slave shows the agony of that process and the ecstasy of the result.

▶ *Tour over! These two may be slaves of the museum, but you are free to go. You've seen the essential Louvre. To leave the museum, turn right and follow signs down the stairs to the* Sortie.

Orsay Museum Tour

Musée d'Orsay

The Musée d'Orsay (mew-zay dor-say), housing French art from 1848-1914, picks up where the Louvre's art collection leaves off. That means Impressionism, the art of sun-dappled fields, bright colors, and crowded Parisian cafés. The Orsay houses the best general collection anywhere of Manet, Monet, Renoir, Degas, Van Gogh, Cézanne, and Gauguin. If you like Impressionism, visit this museum. If you don't like Impressionism, visit this museum. I find it a more enjoyable and rewarding place than the Louvre. Sure, ya gotta see the *Mona Lisa* and *Venus de Milo,* but after you get your gottas out of the way, enjoy the Orsay.

ORIENTATION

Cost: €16, free on first Sun of month, covered by Museum Pass; combo-tickets with the Orangerie (€18) or Rodin Museum (€24) are sold only at those museums—not at the Orsay; keep ticket for discount at the Opéra Garnier.

Hours: Tue-Sun 9:30-18:00, Thu until 21:45, closed Mon, last entry one hour before closing (45 minutes on Thu). The top-floor Impressionist galleries begin closing 45 minutes early.

Information: +33 1 40 49 48 14, www.musee-orsay.fr.

When to Go: For shorter lines and fewer crowds, visit on Wed, Fri, or Thu evening. It's most crowded on Sun, as well as on Tue, when the Louvre is closed.

Avoiding Lines: Avoid the long ticket-buying lines with a Museum Pass, a combo-ticket, or by purchasing tickets in advance on the Orsay website; any of these entitle you to use a separate entrance.

Tickets and Museum Passes are sold at the newspaper kiosk just outside the Orsay (along Rue de la Légion d'Honneur).

Getting There: The museum sits at 1 Rue de la Légion d'Honneur (Mo: Solférino, RER/Train-C: Musée d'Orsay). From the Louvre, catch bus #69 along Rue de Rivoli, or walk 15 minutes through the Tuileries Garden and across the bridge. A taxi stand is in front on Quai Anatole France, and the Batobus boat stops here.

Getting In: As you face the entrance, pass and ticket holders enter on the right (Entrance C).

Tours: **Audioguides** cost €6. English-language **guided tours** are available; confirm times—usually Mon-Sat at 11:00 (€6/1.5 hours, none on Sun, may also run at 14:30 and Thu at 18:30 in high season).

🎧 Download my free Orsay Museum **audio tour.**

Length of This Tour: Allow two hours. With less time, focus on the Impressionists and Post-Impressionists.

Cuisine Art: The *très* elegant **$$$ Le Restaurant** on the museum's second floor has an affordable afternoon tea and coffee service. Stylish **$$ Café Campana** serves simpler meals to crowds on the fifth floor. Outside several classy eateries line Rue du Bac.

Starring: Manet, Monet, Renoir, Degas, Van Gogh, Cézanne, and Gauguin.

Orsay Museum—Ground Floor

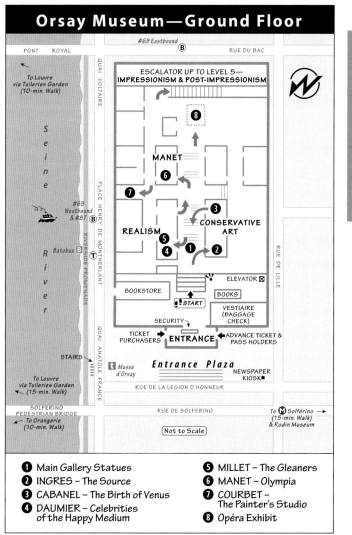

ESCALATOR UP TO LEVEL 5—
IMPRESSIONISM & POST-IMPRESSIONISM

MANET

CONSERVATIVE ART

REALISM

ELEVATOR

BOOKSTORE

BOOKS

START

VESTIAIRE (BAGGAGE CHECK)

SECURITY

TICKET PURCHASERS

ENTRANCE

ADVANCE TICKET & PASS HOLDERS

Musée d'Orsay

Entrance Plaza

NEWSPAPER KIOSK

RUE DE LA LEGION D'HONNEUR

STAIRS

To Louvre via Tuileries Garden (15-min. Walk)

SOLFERINO PEDESTRIAN BRIDGE
To Orangerie (10-min. Walk)

RUE DE SOLFERINO

To Solférino (15-min. Walk) & Rodin Museum

Not to Scale

#69 Eastbound

PONT ROYAL

RUE DU BAC

To Louvre via Tuileries Garden (10-min. Walk)

QUAI VOLTAIRE

Seine River

#69 Westbound & #87

Batobus

PLACE HENRY DE MONTHERLANT

RIVERSIDE PROMENADE

QUAI ANATOLE FRANCE

RUE DE LILLE

❶ Main Gallery Statues

❷ INGRES – The Source

❸ CABANEL – The Birth of Venus

❹ DAUMIER – Celebrities of the Happy Medium

❺ MILLET – The Gleaners

❻ MANET – Olympia

❼ COURBET – The Painter's Studio

❽ Opéra Exhibit

THE TOUR BEGINS

▶ *Pick up a free map and belly up to the stone balustrade overlooking the ground floor.*

Trains used to run right under our feet down the center of the gallery. This former train station, the Gare d'Orsay, barely escaped the wrecking ball in the 1970s, when the French realized it'd be a great place to house the enormous collections of 19th-century art scattered throughout the city.

From this perch, survey our tour route. We'll do two laps around three floors of this grand museum: Stretching before you on the ground floor is conservative art of the Academy and Salon, with some early rebels mixed in. At the far end, we'll ride escalators to the top floor, where we'll enjoy the Impressionists and Post-Impressionists like Van Gogh (if you're pressed for time, go directly there). Then, we'll descend to the mezzanine level for a wander through Rodin's statues and some prime examples of Art Nouveau. Ready? *Bien.*

The museum rotates its large collection often, so use your Orsay map and be ready to go with the flow.

▶ *Walk down the steps to the main floor, a gallery filled with statues.*

Conservative Art

Main Gallery Statues

No, this isn't ancient Greece. These statues are from the same era as the Theory of Relativity. It's the conservative art of the French schools, and it was very popular for its beauty—balanced poses, perfect anatomy, sweet faces, curving lines, and gleaming white stone.

The Orsay's main hall—former train station

Ingres' *Source*—clean, sculptural lines

The Orsay's "19th Century" (1848-1914)

Einstein and Geronimo. Abraham Lincoln and Karl Marx. The train, the bicycle, the horse and buggy, the automobile, and the balloon. Freud and Dickens. Darwin's *Origin of Species* and the Church's Immaculate Conception. Louis Pasteur and Billy the Kid. Ty Cobb and V. I. Lenin.

The 19th century was a mix of old and new, side by side. Europe was entering the modern Industrial Age, with cities, factories, rapid transit, instant communication, and global networks. At the same time, it clung to the past with traditional, rural—almost medieval—attitudes and morals.

According to the Orsay, the "19th century" began in 1848 with the socialist and democratic revolutions (Marx's *Communist Manifesto*). It ended in 1914 with the pull of an assassin's trigger, which ignited World War I and ushered in the modern world. The museum shows art that is also both old and new, conservative and revolutionary.

(I'll bad-mouth it later, but for now appreciate the exquisite craftsmanship of this "perfect" art.)

▶ *Take a right into the small Room 1, marked* Ingres, Delacroix, Chassériau. *Look for a nude woman with a pitcher of water.*

Ingres, *The Source (La Source)*, 1856

Let's start where the Louvre left off. Jean-Auguste-Dominique Ingres (ang-gruh), who helped cap the Louvre collection, championed a Neoclassical style. *The Source* is virtually a Greek statue on canvas. Her skin is porcelain-smooth, painted with seamless brushstrokes.

Ingres worked on this painting over the course of 35 years and considered it his "image of perfection." Famous in its day, *The Source* influenced many artists whose classical statues and paintings are in this museum.

In the Orsay's first few rooms, you're surrounded by visions of idealized beauty—nude women in languid poses, Greek mythological figures, and anatomically perfect statues. This was the art adored by French academics and the middle-class (*bourgeois*) public. The 19th-century art world was dominated by two conservative institutions: the Academy (the state-funded art school) and the Salon, where works were exhibited to the buying public. The art they produced was technically perfect, refined, uplifting, and heroic. Some might even say...boring.

▶ *Continue to Room 3 to find a pastel blue-green painting of a swooning Venus.*

Cabanel, *The Birth of Venus* (*La Naissance de Vénus*), 1863

Cabanel lays Ingres' *The Source* on her back. This goddess is a perfect fantasy, an orgasm of beauty. The Love Goddess stretches back seductively, recently birthed from the ephemeral foam of the waves. This is art of a pre-Freudian society, when sex was dirty and mysterious and had to be exalted into a more pure and divine form. French folk would literally swoon in ecstasy before these works of art. Like it? Go ahead, swoon. If it feels good, enjoy it. (If you feel guilty, get over it.) Now, take a mental cold shower, and get ready for a Realist's view.

▶ *Cross the main gallery of statues, backtrack toward the entrance, and enter Room 4 (directly across from Ingres), marked* Daumier.

Realism, Early Rebels, and the Belle Epoque

Daumier, *Celebrities of the Happy Medium* (*Célébrités du Juste Milieu*), 1832-1835

This is a liberal's look at the stuffy bourgeois establishment that controlled the Academy and the Salon. In these 36 bustlets, Honoré Daumier, trained as a political cartoonist, exaggerates each subject's most distinct characteristic to capture with vicious precision the pomposity and self-righteousness of these self-appointed arbiters of taste. Daumier gave insulting nicknames for the person being caricatured, like "gross, fat, and satisfied" or Monsieur "Platehead." Give a few nicknames yourself. Can you find Reagan, Clinton, Kerry, Sarkozy, Al Sharpton, Gingrich, Trump, and Paul Ryan with sideburns? How about Margaret Thatcher...or is that a dude?

These people hated the art you're about to see. Their prudish faces tightened as their fantasy world was shattered by the Realists.

▶ *Nearby, find Millet's* Gleaners.

Cabanel's *Venus*—soft-porn fantasy

Millet's *Gleaners*—hard-core Realism

Millet, *The Gleaners (Les Glaneuses)*, 1867

Jean-François Millet (mee-yay) shows us three gleaners, the poor women who pick up the meager leftovers after a field has already been harvested for the wealthy. Millet grew up on a humble farm. He didn't attend the Academy and despised the uppity Paris art scene. Instead of idealized gods, goddesses, nymphs, and winged babies, he painted simple rural scenes. He was strongly affected by the socialist revolution of 1848, with its affirmation of the working class. Here he captures the innate dignity of these stocky, tanned women who bend their backs quietly in a large field for their small reward.

This is "Realism" in two senses. It's painted "realistically," not prettified. And it's the "real" world—not the fantasy world of Greek myth, but the harsh life of the working poor.

▶ *For a Realist's take on the traditional Venus, walk farther up the gallery and find Manet's* Olympia *in Room 14.*

Manet, *Olympia*, 1863

"This brunette is thoroughly ugly. Her face is stupid, her skin cadaverous. All this clash of colors is stupefying." So wrote a critic when Edouard Manet's nude hung in the Salon. The public hated it, attacking Manet (man-ay) in print and literally attacking the canvas.

Compare this uncompromising nude with Cabanel's idealized, pastel, Vaseline-on-the-lens beauty in *The Birth of Venus*. Cabanel's depiction was basically soft-core pornography, the kind you see today selling lingerie and perfume.

Manet's nude doesn't gloss over anything. The pose is classic, used by Titian, Goya, and countless others. But the traditional pose is challenged by the model's jarring frankness. The sharp outlines and

Manet's *Olympia* shocked the public, mixing a classic pose with modern frankness.

harsh, contrasting colors are new and shocking. Her hand is a clamp, and her stare is shockingly defiant, with not a hint of the seductive, hey-sailor look of most nudes. This prostitute, ignoring the flowers sent by her last customer, looks out as if to say, "Next." Manet replaced soft-core porn with hard-core art.

▶ *Exit Room 14 up a few steps, hook left, and then right to see a huge canvas at the end of a large open space...*

Courbet, *The Painter's Studio (L'Atelier du Peintre)*, 1855

The Salon of 1855 rejected this dark-colored, sprawling, monumental painting that perplexed casual viewers. In an age when "Realist painter" was equated with "bomb-throwing Socialist," it took courage to buck the system. Dismissed by the so-called experts, Gustave Courbet (coor-bay) held his own one-man exhibit. He built a shed in the middle of Paris, defiantly hung his art out, and basically mooned the shocked public.

Courbet's painting takes us backstage, showing us the gritty reality behind the creation of pretty pictures. We see Courbet himself in his studio, working diligently on a Realistic landscape, oblivious to the confusion around him. Milling around are ordinary citizens, not Greek heroes. The woman who looks on is not a nude Venus but

Courbet—behind the scenes at his studio

"Grr. I hate Impressionism."

a naked artist's model. And the little boy with an adoring look on his face? Perhaps it's Courbet's inner child, admiring the artist who sticks to his guns, whether it's popular or not.

▶ *Return to the main corridor, turn left and head to the far end of the gallery, where you'll walk on a glass floor over a model of Paris.*

Opéra Exhibit

Expand to 100 times your size and hover over this scale-model section of the city. In the center sits the 19th-century Opéra Garnier, with its green-domed roof. Nearby, you'll also see a cross-section model of the Opéra and models of set designs from some famous productions. The Opéra Garnier—opened in 1875—was the symbol of the belle époque, or "beautiful age." Paris was a global center of prosperity, new technology, opera, ballet, painting, and joie de vivre. But behind Paris' gilded and gas-lit exterior, a counterculture simmered.

▶ *Take the escalator up to the top floor (follow signs for 5th floor and Impressionisme). Pause to take in a commanding **view** of the vast interior of the Orsay. Follow the crowds and enter the Impressionist rooms.*

Impressionism

Light! Color! Vibrations! You don't hang an Impressionist canvas—you tether it. Impressionism features bright colors, easygoing open-air scenes, spontaneity, broad brushstrokes, and the play of light.

The Impressionist collection is scattered chronologically through Rooms 29-36. You'll see Monet hanging in many rooms, Manet sprinkled among Pissarro and Sisley, and a few Renoir here and a lot of

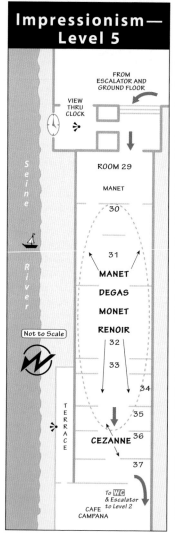

Renoir there. Shadows dance and the displays mingle. Where they're hung is a lot like their brushwork...delightfully sloppy. If you don't see a described painting, just move on.

The Impressionists made their canvases shimmer by using a simple but revolutionary technique. Let's say you mix red, yellow, and green together—you'll get brown, right? But Impressionists didn't bother to mix them. They'd slap a thick brushstroke of yellow down, then a stroke of green next to it, then red next to that. Up close, all you see are the three messy strokes, but as you back up...*voilà!* Brown! The colors blend in the eye, at a distance. But while your eye is saying "bland old brown," your subconscious is shouting, "Red! Yellow! Green! Yes!"

There are no lines in nature, yet someone in the classical tradition (Ingres, for example) would draw an outline of his subject, then fill it in with color. Instead the Impressionists built a figure with dabs of paint...a snowman of color.

Although this top floor displays the Impressionists, you'll find a wide variety of styles. What united these artists was their commitment to everyday subjects (cafés, street scenes, landscapes,

Manet, the mentor of the Impressionists, experimented with open-air painting.

workers), their disdain for the uptight Salon, their love of color, and a sense of artistic rebellion.

The Impressionists all seemed to know each other. You may have seen a group portrait by Henri Fantin-Latour (on the main floor) depicting the circle of Parisian artists and intellectuals. They all learned from each other and taught each other, and they all influenced the next generation's artists (Matisse and Picasso), who created Modern art.

This part of the tour is less a room-by-room itinerary than an introduction to the Orsay's ever-changing collection. Think of it as a sun-dappled treasure hunt.

▶ *Start with the Impressionists' mentor, Manet, whose work is usually found in Room 29.*

Edouard Manet (1832-1883)

Manet had an upper-class upbringing and some formal art training and had been accepted by the Salon. He could have cranked out pretty

Painting "in the Open Air"

The camera threatened to make artists obsolete. Now a machine could capture a better likeness faster than you could say "Etch-a-Sketch."

But true art is more than just painting reality. It gives us reality from the artist's point of view, with the artist's personal impressions of the scene. Impressions are often fleeting, so working quickly is essential.

The Impressionist painters rejected camera-like detail for a quick style more suited to capturing the passing moment. Feeling stifled by the rigid rules and stuffy atmosphere of the Academy, the Impressionists grabbed their berets and scarves and went on excursions to the country, where they set up their easels (and newly invented tubes of premixed paint) on riverbanks and hillsides, or they sketched in cafés and dance halls. Gods, goddesses, nymphs, and fantasy scenes are out; common people and rural landscapes were in.

The quick style and everyday subjects were ridiculed and called childish by the "experts." Rejected by the Salon, the Impressionists staged their own exhibition in 1874. They brashly took their name from an insult thrown at them by a critic who laughed at one of Monet's "impressions" of a sunrise. During the next decade, they exhibited their own work independently. The public was slowly won over by the simplicity, the color, and the vibrancy of Impressionist art.

nudes and been a successful painter, but instead he surrounded himself with a group of young artists experimenting with new techniques. His reputation and strong personality made him their master, but he also learned equally from them. Manet's thumbnail bio is typical of almost all the Impressionists: They rejected a "normal" career (lawyer, banker, grocer) to become artists, got classical art training, exhibited in the Salon, became fascinated by Realist subjects, but grew tired of the Salon's dogmatism.

Manet's **Luncheon on the Grass** (*Le Déjeuner sur l'Herbe,* 1863) shocked Paris. The staid citizens looked at this and wondered: What are these scantily clad women doing with these men? Or rather, what will they be doing after the last baguette is eaten? It isn't the nudity, but the presence of the men in ordinary clothes that suddenly makes the nudes look naked. The public judged the painting on moral rather than artistic terms.

A new revolutionary movement was starting to bud—Impressionism. Notice the background: the messy brushwork of trees and leaves, the play of light on the pond, and the light that filters through the trees onto the woman who stoops in the haze. Also note the strong contrast of colors (white skin, black clothes, green grass).

▶ *Scattered in the next galleries are works by two Impressionist masters at their peak, Monet and Renoir (with a bit of Degas in the mix too). You're looking at the quintessence of Impressionism. Monet and Renoir were good friends, often working side-by-side, and their canvases sometimes hang next to each other in these rooms.*

Claude Monet (1840-1926)

Monet (mo-nay) is the father of Impressionism. He fully explored the possibilities of open-air painting and tried to faithfully reproduce nature's colors with bright blobs of paint. Throughout his long career, more than any of his colleagues, Monet stuck to the Impressionist credo of creating objective studies in color and light.

In the 1860s, Monet (along with Renoir) began painting landscapes in the open air. Although Monet did the occasional urban scene, he was most at home in the countryside, painting farms, rivers, trees, and passing clouds. He studied optics and pigments to know just the right colors he needed to reproduce the shimmering quality of reflected light. The key was to work quickly—at that "golden hour" (to use a modern photographer's term) when the light was just right. Then he'd create a fleeting "impression" of the scene.

Monet is known for his series of paintings on the same subject. For example, you may see several canvases of the **cathedral in Rouen.** In 1893, Monet went to Rouen, rented a room across from the cathedral, set up his easel...and waited. He wanted to catch "a series of differing impressions" of the cathedral facade at various times of day and year. He often had several canvases going at once. In all, he did 30 paintings of the cathedral, and each is unique. The time-lapse series shows the sun passing slowly across the sky, creating different-colored light and shadows. The labels next to the art describe the conditions: in gray weather, in the morning, morning sun, full sunlight, and so on.

As Monet zeroed in on the play of colors and light, the physical subject—the cathedral—dissolved. It's only a rack upon which to hang the light and color.

Monet's cathedral dissolves into a pattern of paint, pointing the way toward purely abstract art.

Renoir—in this scene from Montmartre—captures the joie de vivre of the belle époque.

One of Monet's favorite places to paint was the garden he landscaped at his home in **Giverny,** west of Paris (and worth a visit, provided you like Monet more than you hate crowds). The Japanese bridge and the water lilies floating in the pond were his two favorite subjects. As Monet aged and his eyesight failed, he made bigger canvases of smaller subjects. The final water lilies (at the Orangerie and Marmottan museums) are monumental smudges of thick paint surrounded by paint-splotched clouds that are reflected on the surface of the pond.

Pierre-Auguste Renoir (1841-1919)

Renoir (ren-wah) started out as a painter of landscapes, along with Monet, but later veered from the Impressionist's philosophy and painted images that were unabashedly "pretty." He populated his canvases with rosy-cheeked, middle-class girls performing happy domestic activities, rendered in a warm, inviting style. As Renoir himself said, "There are enough ugly things in life."

Renoir's lighthearted work uses light colors—no brown or black.

The paint is thin and translucent, and the outlines are soft, so the figures blend seamlessly with the background. He seems to be searching for an ideal, the sort of pure beauty we saw in paintings on the ground floor.

In his last years (confined to a wheelchair with arthritis), Renoir turned to full-figured nudes—like those painted by Old Masters such as Rubens or Boucher. He introduced more and more red tones, as if trying for even greater warmth.

Renoir's best-known work is **Dance at the Moulin de la Galette** (*Bal du Moulin de la Galette,* 1876). On Sunday afternoons, working-class folk would dress up and head for the fields on Butte Montmartre (near Sacré-Cœur basilica) to dance, drink, and eat little crêpes (galettes) till dark. Renoir liked to go there to paint the common Parisians living and loving in the afternoon sun. The sunlight filtering through the trees creates a kaleidoscope of colors, like the 19th-century equivalent of a mirror ball throwing darts of light onto the dancers.

He captured the dappled light with quick blobs of yellow staining the ground, the men's jackets, and the sun-dappled straw hat (right of center). The painting glows with bright colors. Even the shadows on the ground, which should be gray or black, are colored a warm blue. Like a photographer who uses a slow shutter speed to show motion, Renoir paints a waltzing blur.

Edgar Degas (1834-1917)

Degas (day-gah) was a rich kid from a family of bankers, and he got the best classical-style art training. He painted in the Academic style, exhibited in the Salon, gained a good reputation, and then...he met the Impressionists.

Degas blends classical lines and Realist subjects with Impressionist color, spontaneity, and everyday scenes from urban Paris. He loved the unposed "snapshot" effect, catching his models off guard. Dance students, women at work, and café scenes are approached from odd angles that aren't always ideal but make the scenes seem more real. He gives us the backstage view of life.

Degas loved dance and the theater. The play of stage lights off his dancers, especially the halos of ballet skirts, is made to order for an Impressionist. A dance rehearsal let Degas capture a behind-the-scenes look at bored, tired, restless dancers (**The Dance Class,** *La Classe de Danse,* c. 1873-1875). Pirouetting near his oil paintings of

Monet—the Japanese Bridge at Giverny

Degas—behind-the-scenes look at dancers

dancers, you'll see his small and life-size statues of them—he first modeled the figures in wax, then cast them in bronze.

Degas hung out with low-life Impressionists, discussing art, love, and life in the cheap cafés and bars in Montmartre. In the painting ***In a Café*** (*Dans un Café,* 1875-1876), a weary lady of the evening meets morning with a last, lonely, nail-in-the-coffin drink in the glaring light of a four-in-the-morning café. The pale green drink at the center of the composition is the toxic substance absinthe, which fueled many artists and burned out many more.

Camille Pissarro, Alfred Sisley, and Others

The Orsay features some of the "lesser" pioneers of the Impressionist style. Browse around and discover your own favorites. Pissarro is one of mine. His grainy landscapes are more subtle and subdued than those of the flashy Monet and Renoir—but, as someone said, "He did for the earth what Monet did for the water."

Paul Cézanne (1839-1906)

Paul Cézanne (say-zahn) brought Impressionism into the 20th century. After the color of Monet and the warmth of Renoir, Cézanne's rather impersonal canvases can be difficult to appreciate. Bowls of fruit, landscapes, and a few portraits were Cézanne's passion (see ***The Card Players,*** *Les Joueurs de Cartes,* 1890-1895). Because of his style (not the content), he is often called the first modern painter.

Cézanne was virtually unknown and unappreciated in his lifetime. He worked alone, lived alone, and died alone, ignored by all but a few revolutionary young artists who understood his genius.

Unlike the Impressionists, who painted what they saw, Cézanne reworked reality. He simplified it into basic geometric forms—circular

Degas took "snapshots" of ordinary people—at work, at the theater, or in a late-night café.

apples, rectangular boulders, cone-shaped trees, triangular groups of people. He might depict a scene from multiple angles—showing a tabletop from above but the bowl of fruit resting on it from the side. He laid paint down with heavy brushstrokes, blending the background and foreground to obliterate traditional 3-D depth. He worked slowly, methodically, stroke by stroke—a single canvas could take months.

Where the Impressionists built a figure out of a mosaic of individual brushstrokes, Cézanne used blocks of paint to create a more solid, geometrical shape. These chunks are like little "cubes." It's no coincidence that his experiments in reducing forms to their geometric basics inspired the...Cubists.

Taking Cézanne's "slabism" a step further, the last room in this gallery is dedicated to Pointillism and the vibrant dots of Seurat and Signac.

▶ *Break time. Try the jazzy Café Campana or venture out on the terrace for fresh air and great views. WCs are nearby (upstairs on level 6).*

Cezanne built this scene out of patches of paint, anticipating the "cubes" of Cubism.

Post-Impressionism

The Impressionists were like a tribe. They spoke the same artistic language. But, after that, more than ever, artists went in different directions, creating art that was uniquely their own. Van Gogh, Gauguin, and Toulouse-Lautrec are fine examples of these Post-Impressionists, and their paintings line the walls of the next string of rooms (Rooms 43-45 especially).

▶ *You'll find the Post-Impressionists in a series of rooms behind the café. Just follow the signs to Van Gogh.*

Vincent van Gogh (1853-1890)

Impressionists have been accused of being "light"-weights. The colorful style lends itself to bright country scenes, gardens, sunlight on the water, and happy crowds of simple people. It took a remarkable genius to add profound emotion to the Impressionist style.

Like Michelangelo, Beethoven, and a select handful of others, Vincent van Gogh (pronounced "van-go," or van-HOCK by the Dutch and the snooty) put so much of himself into his work that art and life

Post-Impressionism—Level 5

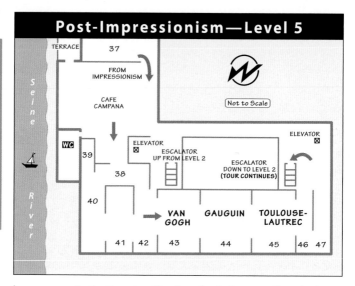

became one. In the Orsay's collection of paintings, you'll see both Van Gogh's painting style and his life unfold.

Vincent was the son of a Dutch minister. He too felt a religious calling, and he spread the gospel among the poorest of the poor—peasants and miners in overcast Holland and Belgium. He painted these hardworking, dignified folks in a crude, dark style reflecting the oppressiveness of their lives...and his own loneliness as he roamed northern Europe in search of a calling.

Encouraged by his art-dealer brother, Van Gogh moved to Paris, and *voilà!* The color! He met Monet, drank with Gauguin and Toulouse-Lautrec, and soaked up the Impressionist style. (For example, see how he might build a bristling brown beard using thick strokes of red, yellow, and green side by side.)

At first, he painted like the others, but soon he developed his own style. Van Gogh's brushstrokes curve and thrash like a garden hose pumped with wine.

The social life of Paris became too much for the solitary Van Gogh, and he moved to the south of France. At first, in the glow of the bright spring sunshine, he had a period of incredible creativity and

Van Gogh's *Midday, La Méridienne*—painted during a happy time in the south of France

happiness. He was overwhelmed by the bright colors, landscape vistas, and common people. It was an Impressionist's dream (see **Midday, La Méridienne**, 1889-90).

But being alone in a strange country began to wear on him. An ugly man, he found it hard to get a date. A painting of his rented bedroom in Arles shows a cramped, bare-bones place (**Van Gogh's Bedroom in Arles**, *La Chambre de Van Gogh à Arles*, 1889). He invited his friend Gauguin to join him, but after two months together arguing passionately about art, nerves got raw. Van Gogh threatened Gauguin with a razor, which drove his friend back to Paris. In crazed despair, Van Gogh cut off a piece of his own ear.

The people of Arles realized they had a madman on their hands and convinced Vincent to seek help at a mental hospital. The paintings he finished in the peace of the hospital are more meditative—there are fewer bright landscapes and more closed-in scenes with deeper, almost surreal colors.

Van Gogh, the preacher's son, saw painting as a calling, and he

In Van Gogh's *Self-Portrait*, the swirl of brushstrokes captures the artist's restless energy.

approached it with a spiritual intensity. In his last days, he wavered between happiness and madness. He despaired of ever being sane enough to continue painting.

His final self-portrait shows a man engulfed in a confused background of brushstrokes that swirl and rave (**Self-Portrait,** *Portrait de l'Artiste,* 1889). But in the midst of this rippling sea of mystery floats a still, detached island of a face. Perhaps his troubled eyes know that in only a few months, he'll take a pistol and put a bullet through his chest.

▶ *Carry on to the next room, where you'll find works by...*

Paul Gauguin (1848-1903)

Gauguin (go-gan) got the travel bug early in childhood and grew up wanting to be a sailor. Instead, he became a stockbroker. In his spare time, he painted, and he was introduced to the Impressionist circle. He learned their bright clashing colors but diverged from their path about the time Van Gogh waved a knife in his face. At the age of 35, he got fed up with it all, quit his job, abandoned his wife and family, and took refuge in his art. (Look for his self-portrait with the travel-dreams background.)

Gauguin's *Arearea* shows off his childlike use of bright blocks of color.

Gauguin traveled to the South Seas in search of the exotic, finally settling on Tahiti. There he found his Garden of Eden. He simplified his life into a routine of eating, sleeping, and painting. He simplified his paintings still more, to flat images with heavy black outlines filled with bright, pure colors. The background and foreground colors are equally bright, producing a flat, stained-glass-like surface.

Gauguin's best-known works capture an idyllic Tahitian landscape peopled by exotic women engaged in simple tasks and making music (***Arearea,*** 1892). The local girls lounge placidly in unselfconscious innocence (so different from Cabanel's seductive, melodramatic *Venus*). The style is intentionally "primitive," collapsing the three-dimensional landscape into a two-dimensional pattern of bright colors. Gauguin intended that this simple style carry a deep undercurrent of symbolic meaning. He wanted to communicate to his "civilized" colleagues back home that he'd found the paradise he'd always envisioned.

Van Gogh's room at Arles

▶ *The next section features an artist who found his travel thrills closer to home, in the Paris underworld.*

Henri de Toulouse-Lautrec (1864-1901)

Henri de Toulouse-Lautrec was the black sheep of a noble family. At age 14 he broke both legs, which left him with a normal-size torso but dwarf-size limbs. Shunned by his family, a freak to society, he felt more at home in the world of other outcasts—prostitutes, drunks, thieves, dancers, and actors. He settled in Montmartre, where he painted the life he lived. He drank absinthe and hung out with Van Gogh. He carried a hollow cane filled with booze. When the Moulin Rouge nightclub opened, Henri was hired to do its posters. Every night, the artist put on his bowler hat and visited the Moulin Rouge to draw the crowds, the can-can dancers, and the backstage action. Toulouse-Lautrec died at age 36 of syphilis and alcoholism.

Toulouse-Lautrec's painting style captures Realist scenes with strong, curvaceous outlines. He worked quickly, creating sketches in paint that serve as snapshots of a golden era.

In *Jane Avril Dancing* (*Jane Avril Dansant,* 1891), he depicts the slim, graceful, elegant, and melancholy dancer, who stood out above the rabble. Her legs keep dancing while her mind is far away. Toulouse-Lautrec, the "artistocrat," might have identified with her noble face—sad and weary of the nightlife, but immersed in it.

▶ *Now ride the escalator down to level 2, an open-air mezzanine lined with statues. Make a circle around the mezzanine as you enjoy the work of Rodin, Claudel, and their contemporaries.*

French Sculpture
This section is frequently shuffled about. You should find most of these works close by, though some may be away for restoration.

Auguste Rodin (1840-1917)
Born of working-class roots and largely self-taught, Rodin combined classical solidity with Impressionist surfaces to become the greatest sculptor since Michelangelo. He labored in obscurity for decades, making knickknacks and doorknobs for a construction company. By age 40, he started to gain recognition.

Like his statue of *The Walking Man* (*L'Homme Qui Marche,* 1905), Rodin had one foot in the past and one stepping boldly into the future. This muscular, forcefully striding man could be a symbol of the Renaissance Man with his classical power. With no mouth or hands, he speaks with his body. Get close and look at the statue's surface. It's alive, rippling with frosting-like gouges. This rough, "unfinished" look reflects light like the rough Impressionist brushwork. And that makes the statue come to life, never quite at rest in the viewer's eye. Rodin's subject was always the human body, showing it in unusual poses that express inner emotion.

Another good example of Rodin's style is *St. John the Baptist* (*Saint Jean-Baptiste,* 1878), which captures the mystical visionary who was the forerunner of Christ. Rodin's inspiration was a shaggy peasant—looking for work as a model—whose bearing caught the artist's eye. Coarse and hairy, with both feet planted firmly in mid-stride, this sculpture challenged the traditional poses expected from

Rodin worked in bronze, so there are authorized versions of this work elsewhere.

Claudel was dumped by Rodin.

Salle des Fêtes (Grand Ballroom)

a 19th-century artist. A sense of movement and spontaneity mattered more to Rodin than mimicking classical stances.

▶ *Pass a few more works by Rodin before landing (toward the far end of the mezzanine) on a deeply bronzed sculpture with three figures.*

Camille Claudel (1864-1943)

Claudel was Rodin's student, mistress, and muse. In **Maturity** (*L'Age Mur,* c. 1902)—a small bronze statue group of three figures—Claudel may have portrayed their doomed love affair. A young girl desperately reaches out to an older man, who is led away reluctantly by an older woman. The center of the composition is the empty space left when their hands separate. In real life, Rodin refused to leave his wife, and Claudel ended up in an insane asylum.

▶ *At the far end of the hall (hooking left, around the corner), you will run into a large gate cluttered with sculptural brilliance...*

Rodin, *The Gates of Hell* (*La Porte de l'Enfer*), 1880-1917

Rodin worked for decades on this model for a ceremonial "door" depicting the lost souls of Dante's hell. It contains some of his greatest hits—small statues that he later executed in full size. Find *The Thinker* squatting above the doorway, contemplating Man's fate. The door's 186 figures eventually inspired larger versions of *The Kiss,* the *Three Shades,* and more.

From this perch in the Orsay, look down to the main floor at all the classical statues between you and the big clock, and realize how far we've come—not in years, but in stylistic changes. Many of the statues below—beautiful, smooth, balanced, and idealized—were created at the same time as Rodin's powerful, haunting works. Rodin's

One last look—at the main floor, the mezzanine, and the great art we've seen on this tour

sculptures capture the groundbreaking spirit of much of the art in the Orsay Museum. With a stable base of 19th-century stone, he launched art into the 20th century.

▶ *You've seen the essential Orsay and are permitted to cut out. But with extra time, there's an "other" Orsay. The beauty of the Orsay is that it combines all the art from 1848 to 1914, both modern and classical, in one building.*

Rooms 61-66 are a curvaceous IKEA of Art Nouveau furniture. Rooms 55 and 59 feature some non-Impressionist art. The chandeliered Salle des Fêtes (Room 51) was once one of Paris' poshest nightspots. Is this stuff beautiful or merely gaudy? Divine or decadent? Whatever you decide, it was all part of the marvelous world of the Orsay's century of art.

Eiffel Tower Tour

La Tour Eiffel

It's crowded, expensive, and there are probably better views in Paris, but visiting this 1,000-foot-tall ornament is worth the trouble. Visitors to Paris may find *Mona Lisa* to be less than expected, but the Eiffel Tower rarely disappoints, even in an era of skyscrapers. This is a once-in-a-lifetime, I've-been-there experience. Making the eye-popping ascent and ear-popping descent gives you membership into the exclusive society of the quarter of a billion other humans who have made the Eiffel Tower the most visited monument in the modern world.

ORIENTATION

Cost: €27 to ride to the top (third) level, €17.50 to ride to the first or second level, €11 to climb the stairs to the first or second level, €21 to take the stairs and then elevator to the summit—must purchase summit elevator before entering tower, not covered by Museum Pass.

Hours: Daily mid-June-Aug 9:00-24:45, Sept-mid-June 9:30-23:45, last ascent to top by elevator at 22:30 and to lower levels at 23:00 all year (stairs same except Sept-mid-June last ascent 18:30). The top level can close temporarily in windy weather. If you've purchased a ticket to the top, you will be allowed to go unless the weather is dangerous.

Information: www.toureiffel.paris.

Advance Tickets Recommended: If you plan to ascend by elevator, it's strongly advised to book a reservation online (any ticket that includes the stairs can only be purchased on-site). Booking online allows you to reserve an entry time and skip the (usually long) ticket-buying line at no extra cost.

Online ticket sales open up 60 days before any given date (at 8:30 Paris time)—and can quickly sell out (especially for April-Sept). If no slots are available, try buying a "Lift entrance ticket with access to 2nd floor"—the view from the second floor is arguably better anyway. Or, try the website again about a week before your visit. To go all the way to the top, select "Lift entrance ticket with access to the summit."

Buying Tickets On-Site: On occasion it's possible to just drop by, buy a ticket, and go directly up the tower. But you're much more

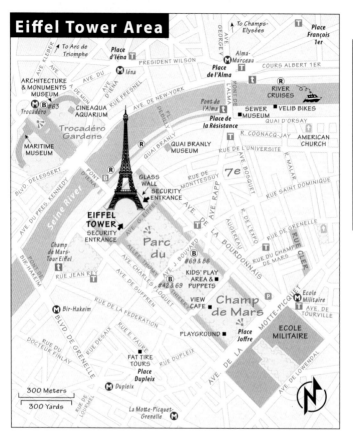

likely to find yourself in horrible lines. Weekends and holidays are worst. If you don't have a reservation, arrive at least 30 minutes before the tower opens to pass security (security opens 30 minutes before the tower), then immediately get in line to buy a ticket. Going much later in the day is the next-best bet (after 19:00 May-Aug, after 17:00 off-season, after 16:00 in winter as it gets dark by 17:00).

When to Go: For the best of all worlds, arrive with enough light to see the views, then stay as it gets dark to see the lights.

Getting There: The tower is about a 10-minute walk from the Métro (Bir-Hakeim or Trocadéro stops) or suburban train (RER/Train-C Champ de Mars-Tour Eiffel stop). The Ecole Militaire Métro stop in the Rue Cler area is 20 minutes away. Buses #42, #69, and #86 stop nearby.

Getting In: For security, the perimeter of the tower is surrounded by glass walls. So, while it's free to enter the area directly under the tower, to do so you must pass through an airport-like **security check** (allow 30 minutes or more at busy times).

    If you have a reservation, arrive at the tower at least 30 minutes before your entry time. Once you're through security, look for an entrance with green signs showing *Visiteurs avec Reservation* (Visitors with Reservation).

    Without an elevator reservation, after passing security, go directly to the yellow-bannered ticket booth (follow signs for *Individuels* or *Visiteurs sans Tickets*).

    Stair walkers buy their tickets directly at the south pillar, which is for stair access only.

Length of This Tour: If you have reservations and crowds are light, you can get to the top and back (with minimal sightseeing) in 90 minutes. Otherwise, budget three to four hours to wait in line, get to the top, and sightsee your way back down.

Security Check: Bags larger than 19" × 8" × 12" are not allowed, and there is no baggage check.

Services: Free WCs are at the base of the tower, behind the east pillar. Inside the tower itself, WCs are on all levels, but have long lines.

Eating: The tower's two classy **$$$$** restaurants offer great views, and a reservation at either one lets you skip the initial elevator line (book well in advance). You can't skip security lines and you can't ascend more than 15-30 minutes prior to your reservation time (though you can linger afterward). On the first level is **58 Tour Eiffel** (+33 1 72 76 18 46, www.restaurants-toureiffel.com). The more expensive **Le Jules Verne** restaurant is on the second level (+33 1 45 55 61 44, www.lejulesverne-paris.com).

    Consider assembling a picnic beforehand from any of several handy shops near Métro stop Ecole Militaire and eat in the

Champ de Mars park (on the side grassy areas or on benches along the central grass; the middle stretch may be off-limits).

Starring: All of Paris...and beyond.

THE TOUR BEGINS

There are three observation platforms, at roughly 200, 400, and 900 feet. Although being on the windy top of the Eiffel Tower is a thrill you'll never forget, the view is better from the second level, where you can actually see Paris' monuments. All three levels have some displays, WCs, souvenir stores, and a few other services.

For the hardy, stairs lead from the ground level up to the first level (360 steps) and second level (another 360 steps). The staircase is enclosed with a wire cage, so you can't fall, but those with vertigo issues may still find them dizzying.

If you want to see the entire tower, from top to bottom, then see it...from top to bottom. There isn't a single elevator straight to the top (*le sommet*). To get there, you'll first ride an elevator (or hike up the stairs) to the second level. (Some elevators stop on the first level, but it's more efficient to see the first level on the way down). Once on the second level, immediately line up for the next elevator, to the top. Enjoy the views from the "summit," then ride back down to the second level. Frolic there for a while, then head to the first level via the stairs (no line and can take as little as five minutes) and explore the shops and exhibits. To leave, you can line up for the elevator, but it's quickest and most memorable to take the stairs back down to earth.

Exterior

Delicate and graceful when seen from afar, the Eiffel Tower is massive—even a bit scary—close up. You don't appreciate its size until you walk toward it; like a mountain, it seems so close but takes forever to reach.

The tower, including its antenna, stands 1,063 feet tall, or slightly higher than the 77-story Chrysler Building in New York. Its four support pillars straddle an area of 3.5 acres. Despite the tower's 7,300 tons of metal and 60 tons of paint, it is so well engineered that it weighs no more per square inch at its base than a linebacker on tiptoes.

Once the world's tallest structure, it's now eclipsed by a number

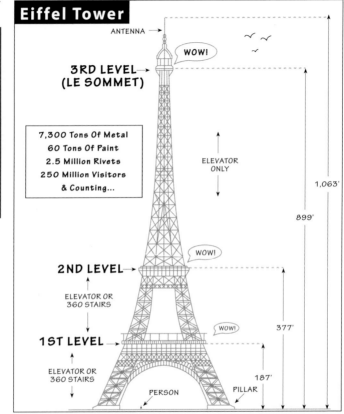

Eiffel Tower

ANTENNA

WOW!

3RD LEVEL (LE SOMMET)

7,300 Tons Of Metal
60 Tons Of Paint
2.5 Million Rivets
250 Million Visitors
& Counting...

ELEVATOR ONLY

1,063'

899'

WOW!

2ND LEVEL

ELEVATOR OR 360 STAIRS

WOW!

377'

1ST LEVEL

ELEVATOR OR 360 STAIRS

187'

PERSON

PILLAR

of towers (Tokyo Skytree, 2,080 feet, for one), radio antennae (KVLY-TV mast, North Dakota, 2,063 feet), and skyscrapers (Burj Khalifa in Dubai, UAE, 2,717 feet).

The long green lawn stretching south of the tower is the Champ de Mars, originally the training ground for troops and students of the nearby military school (Ecole Militaire) and now a park. On the north side, across the Seine, is the curved palace colonnade framing a square called the Trocadéro.

Up and Down

The tower—which was designed from the start to accommodate hordes of visitors—has always had elevators. Back in the late 19th century, elevator technology was so new that they needed a special design to accommodate the angle of the tower's pillars. Today's elevators (modern replacements) make about 100 round-trip journeys a day.

There are 1,665 stairs to the top level, though tourists can only climb 720 of them, up as far as the second level. During a race in 1905, a gentleman climbed from the ground to the second level—elevation gain nearly 400 feet—in 3 minutes, 12 seconds.

History

The first visitor to the Paris World's Fair in 1889 walked beneath the "arch" formed by the newly built Eiffel Tower and entered the fairgrounds. This event celebrated both the centennial of the French Revolution and France's position as a global superpower. Bridge builder Gustave Eiffel (1832-1923) won the contest to build the fair's centerpiece by beating out rival proposals such as a giant guillotine.

Eiffel deserved to have the tower named for him. He not only designed it, he financed it, his factory produced the iron beams, he designed special cranes and apparatus to build it, and—working on a deadline for the World's Fair—he brought in the project on time and under budget.

The tower was nothing but a showpiece, with no functional purpose except to demonstrate to the world that France had the wealth, knowledge, and can-do spirit to erect a structure far taller than anything the world had ever seen. The original plan was to dismantle the

Eiffel—designer, financier, and builder

Wheels turn cables to lift the elevator.

tower as quickly as it was built after the celebration ended, but it was kept by popular demand.

To a generation hooked on technology, the tower was the marvel of the age, a symbol of progress and human ingenuity. Not all were so impressed, however; many found it a monstrosity. The writer Guy de Maupassant (1850-1893) routinely ate lunch in the tower just so he wouldn't have to look at it.

In subsequent years, the tower has come to serve many functions: as a radio transmitter (1909-present), a cosmic-ray observatory (1910), a billboard (spelling "Citroën" in lights, 1925-1934), a broadcaster of Nazi TV programs (1940-1944), a fireworks launch pad (numerous times), and a framework for dazzling lighting displays, including the current arrangement, designed in 2000 for the celebration of the millennium.

▶ *To reach the top, ride the elevator or walk to the second level. From there, get in line for the next elevator and continue to the top. Pop out 900 feet above the ground.*

Third Level (*Le Sommet*)

You'll find wind and grand, sweeping views on the tiny top level. The city lies before you (pick out sights with the help of the panoramic maps). On a good day, you can see for 40 miles. Do a 360-degree tour of Paris.

Looking west (*ouest*): The Seine runs east to west (though at this point it's flowing more southwest). At the far end of the skinny "island" in the river, find the tiny copy of the Statue of Liberty, looking 3,633 miles away to her big sister in New York. Gustave Eiffel, a man of many talents, also designed the internal supports of New York's Statue

Building the Tower

As you ascend through the metal beams, imagine being a worker, perched high above nothing, riveting this thing together. It was a massive project, and it took all the ingenuity of the Industrial Age—including mass production, cutting-edge technology, and capitalist funding.

An 18,000-piece Erector set

The tower went up like an 18,000-piece Erector set, made of 15-foot iron beams held together with 2.5 million rivets. For two years, 300 workers assembled the pieces, the tower rising as they went.

First, they used wooden scaffolding to support the lower (angled) sections, until the pillars came together and the tower could support itself. Then the iron beams were lifted up with steam-powered cranes, including some on tracks (creeper cranes) that inched up the pillars as the tower progressed. There, daring workers dangled from rope ladders, balanced on beams, and tightrope-walked their way across them as they put the pieces in place. The workers then hammered in red-hot rivets made on-site by blacksmiths. As the rivets cooled, they solidified the structure.

After a mere year and a half, the tower surpassed what had been the tallest structure in the world—the Washington Monument (555 feet), which had taken 36 years to build.

The tower was painted a rusty red. Since then, it's sported several colors, including mustard and the current brown-gray. It is repainted every seven years (it takes 25 full-time painters 18 months to apply 60 tons of paint by hand—no spraying allowed).

Two years, two months, and five days after construction began, the tower was done. On May 15, 1889, a red, white, and blue beacon was lit on the top, the World's Fair began, and the tower carried its first astounded visitor to the top.

Looking west—next stop, New York

Looking north—Place Trocadéro

of Liberty, which was cast in copper by fellow Frenchman Frederic Bartholdi (1886).

Looking north (nord): At your feet is the curved arcade of the Trocadéro, itself the site of a World's Fair in 1878. Beyond that is the vast, forested expanse of the Bois de Boulogne, the three-square-mile park that hosts joggers and *boules* players by day and prostitutes by night. In the far distance are the skyscrapers of La Défense and, to the right of the Trocadéro, is the Arc de Triomphe.

Looking east (est): At your feet are the Seine and its many bridges, including the Pont Alexandre, with its four golden statues. Looking farther upstream, find the Orsay Museum, the Louvre, Pont Neuf, and the twin towers of Notre-Dame. On the Right Bank (to your left), is the bullet-shaped dome of Sacré-Cœur, atop Butte Montmartre.

Looking south (sud): In a line, find the Champ de Mars, the Ecole Militaire, the Y-shaped UNESCO building, and the 689-foot Montparnasse Tower skyscraper. To the left is the golden dome of Les Invalides.

The tippy top: Ascend another short staircase to the open-air top, beneath satellite dishes. You'll see the small apartment given to Gustave Eiffel. The mannequins re-create the moment during the 1889 World's Fair when the American Thomas Edison paid a visit to his fellow techie, Gustave and Gustave's daughter Claire, presenting them with his new invention, a phonograph. (Then they cranked it up and blasted The Who's "I Can See for Miles.")

▶ *Ride the elevator down to the…*

Second Level

The second level (400 feet) has the best views because you're closer to the sights, and the monuments are more recognizable. This level has souvenir shops, WCs, and a small stand-up café.

The world-class Le Jules Verne restaurant on this level is currently run by Frédéric Anton, one of the most revered chefs in France today. One would hope his brand of haute cuisine matches the 400-foot haute of the restaurant.

▶ *Catch the elevator or take 360 steps down to the...*

First Level

The first level (200 feet) has more great views, all well described by the tower's panoramic displays. There's really not much here: a small concert hall, a restaurant, and a public hall with a café, shop, and little theater. Pop-up restaurants and kiosks appear with every

The tower is lit from within. At the top of the hour, it sparkles and projects a beacon of light.

season—even a little playground for kids. In winter, part of the first level is often set up to host an ice-skating rink.

The highlight is the breathtaking, vertigo-inducing, selfie-inspiring **glass floor.** Venture onto it and experience what it's like to stand atop an 18-story building and look straight down.

Explore the various exhibits (which change often). You might learn how the sun warms the tower's metal, causing the top to expand and lean about five inches away from the sun, or how the tower oscillates slightly in the wind. Because of its lacy design, even the strongest of winds can't blow the tower down, but only cause it to sway a few inches. In fact, Eiffel designed the tower primarily with wind resistance in mind, wanting a structure seemingly "molded by the action of the wind itself."

▶ *To return to the bottom, take either the elevator or the stairs (five minutes, 360 steps). The stairs are generally much quicker.*

Back on the Ground

Welcome back to earth. For a final look, stroll across the river to Place du Trocadéro or to the end of the Champ de Mars and look back for great views. However impressive it may be by day, the tower is an awesome thing to behold at twilight, when it becomes engorged with light, and virile Paris lies back and lets night be on top. When darkness fully envelops the city, the tower seems to climax with a spectacular light show at the top of each hour...for five glorious minutes.

Rue Cler Walk

The Art of Parisian Living

A stroll down this market street introduces you to a thriving, traditional Parisian neighborhood and its local culture. And although Rue Cler is a wealthy and quickly changing district, it retains an everyday charm still found in most neighborhoods throughout the city.

In food-crazy Paris, shopping for groceries is the backbone of daily life. Rue Cler—traffic-free since 1984—is lined with the essential shops—wine, cheese, chocolate, and bread. To learn the fine art of living Parisian-style, there's no better classroom than Rue Cler. Explore the shops and assemble the ultimate French picnic.

🎧 Download my Rue Cler Walk audio tour.

THE WALK BEGINS

▶ *Start your walk at the northern end of the pedestrian section of Rue Cler, at Rue de Grenelle (right by a bus #69 stop and a short walk from Mo: Ecole Militaire). Visit Rue Cler when its markets are open and lively (Tue-Sat 8:30-13:00 and 15:00-19:30, Sun 8:30-12:00, dead Sun afternoon and Mon). Allow an hour to browse and café-hop along this short, three-block walk. For tips on etiquette when shopping in Paris, see the Shopping section in the Activities chapter.*

❶ Café Roussillon

Standing outside this traditional bar/café, survey the neighborhood. With ground floors devoted to retail and upper floors housing people, there's a vitality here in the middle of a huge metropolis that you don't find in many American cities. Feel the community: people walking dogs, pushing carriages, and dragging shopping carts. Paris is a city of neighborhoods. And this one's equipped with my favorite market street—a traffic-free mall serving this community—Rue Cler.

Café Roussillon, with its traditional bar, is a neighborhood fixture. Cafés like this display a sign, required by French law, making it clear that drinks served at the bar are cheaper than drinks served at the tables. The blackboard lists wines sold by the glass.

▶ *If you're shopping for designer baby clothes, you'll find them across the street at...*

❷ Petit Bateau

The French spend at least as much on their babies as they do on their dogs—dolling them up with designer jammies. This store is one in a popular chain. Little children around here just aren't comfortable unless they're making a fashion statement (such as underwear with sailor stripes).

In the last generation, an aging and shrinking population was a serious problem for Europe's wealthier nations. But France now has one of Europe's biggest baby populations—the French average two children per family, compared to 1.6 for the rest of Europe. Babies are trendy today, and the government rewards parents with big tax incentives for their first two children—and then doubles the incentives after that.

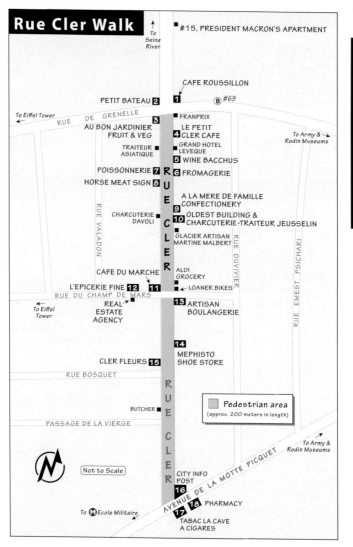

Rue Cler Walk

To Seine River

■ #15, PRESIDENT MACRON'S APARTMENT

CAFE ROUSSILLON

PETIT BATEAU **2**

1

Ⓑ #69

To Eiffel Tower

RUE DE GRENELLE

■ FRANPRIX

3

AU BON JARDINIER
FRUIT & VEG

4 LE PETIT
CLER CAFE

To Army &
Rodin Museums

TRAITEUR
ASIATIQUE ■

■ GRAND HOTEL
LEVEQUE

5 WINE BACCHUS

POISSONNERIE **7** R

6 FROMAGERIE

HORSE MEAT SIGN **8** U

E

■ A LA MERE DE FAMILLE
CONFECTIONERY

9

CHARCUTERIE
DAVOLI ■

C

10 OLDEST BUILDING &
CHARCUTERIE-TRAITEUR JEUSSELIN

L

RUE VALADON

E

GLACIER ARTISAN
MARTINE MALBERT

RUE DUVIVIER

RUE EMEST PSICHARI

R

CAFE DU MARCHE

ALDI
GROCERY

L'EPICERIE FINE **11**

← LOANER BIKES

RUE DU CHAMP DE MARS

To Eiffel
Tower

REAL
ESTATE
AGENCY

13 ARTISAN
BOULANGERIE

14

CLER FLEURS **15**

MEPHISTO
SHOE STORE

RUE BOSQUET

R

U

E

BUTCHER ■

PASSAGE DE LA VIERGE

C

⊠ Pedestrian area
(approx. 200 meters in length)

Ⓝ   Not to Scale

L

E

R

AVENUE DE LA MOTTE PICQUET

To Army &
Rodin Museums

CITY INFO
POST

16

17 18 PHARMACY

To Ⓜ Ecole Militaire

TABAC LA CAVE
A CIGARES

Markets like these continue Rue Cler's long tradition of local produce sellers.

▶ *Cross Rue de Grenelle to find...*

❸ Au Bon Jardinier ("The Good Gardener")
Fruits and Vegetables

Each morning, fresh produce is trucked in from farm fields to Paris' huge Rungis market—Europe's largest, near Orly Airport—and then dispatched to merchants with FedEx-like speed and precision. Good luck finding a shopping bag—locals bring their own two-wheeled carts or reusable bags. The earth-friendly French also resist excessive packaging.

Parisians—who know they eat best by being tuned in to the seasons—shop with their noses. Try it. Smell the cheap foreign strawberries. One sniff of the torpedo-shaped French ones (*gariguettes*), and you know which is better. Locals call those from Belgium "plastic strawberries"—red on the outside, white on the inside. Find the herbs in the back. Is today's delivery in?

The **Franprix** across the street is a small outpost of a nationwide supermarket chain. Opposite Grand Hôtel Lévêque is a ***traiteur asiatique.*** Fast Asian food-to-go—about as common as bakeries—have had an impact on traditional Parisian eating habits.

▶ *Between the Franprix and Grand Hôtel Lévêque is...*

Le French Kiss (*Faire la Bise*)

You can't miss the cheek pecking in Paris. It's contagious—and (even after the pandemic) it's how Parisians greet each other. The lips don't actually touch the cheek—only the cheeks touch, and a gentle kiss noise is made. You usually start by going left (so the right cheeks almost touch), then alternate to the right. The number of times varies with the region or circumstances. Parisians *faire la bise* in social settings but rarely in the workplace. How many kisses are appropriate for an American? If it happens to you, my recommendation is to go for two with confidence, and then—hover and wait.

❹ Le Petit Cler

This small café, a fine choice for a drink or bite with a view, used to be a *tabac* (tobacco shop). It's a good example of how this once working-class market street is becoming increasingly upscale. Some locals regret that these shops are being lost to trendy café crowds.

▶ *Just past Grand Hôtel Lévêque is...*

❺ Wine Bacchus

After they've assembled their meal at other stores, shoppers come here to pick the appropriate wine. Wines are classified by region. Most "Parisians" (born elsewhere) have an affinity for the wines of their home region. You can get a good bottle (especially the wines of the month in the shop's center) for €12. The clerk is a counselor who works with your menu and budget, and they can pop a bottle of white wine into "Le Chiller" and have it cooled for you in three minutes.

▶ *Next door, smell the...*

❻ Fromagerie

Spilling outside into the street, this cheese shop offers more than 200 types of French cheese, both cow (*vache*) and goat (*chèvre*). The place is lab-coat serious but friendly. Known as a *crémerie* or a "BOF," it's where people buy *beurre, oeuf,* and *fromage*—butter, eggs, and cheese.

Notice the many cheese shapes—wedges, cylinders, balls, and miniature hockey pucks all powdered white, gray, and burnt marshmallow. It's a festival of mold. Locals know the shape indicates the

A cheese for nearly every day of the year

Parisians often shop daily.

region of origin (for example, a pyramid shape indicates a cheese from the Loire). And this is important. Regions create the *terroir* (physical and magical union of sun, soil, and generations of farmer love) that gives the product its personality. A Parisian friend once held the stinkiest glob close to her nose, took an orgasmic breath, and exhaled, "Yes, it smells like zee feet of angels."

In the back room, the shop keeps *les meules*—big, 170-pound wheels of cheese, made from 250 gallons of milk. Although you don't eat the skin of these big ones, the skin on most smaller cheeses—the Brie, the Camembert—is part of the taste.

If you order a set *menu* at dinner tonight, you can take the cheese course just before or instead of dessert. On a good cheese plate you have a hard cheese (perhaps a Comté, similar to a white cheddar), a softer cheese (maybe Brie or Camembert), a bleu cheese, and a goat cheese—ideally from different regions. Because it's strongest, the goat cheese is usually eaten last.

▶ *Across the street, find the fish shop.*

❼ Poissonnerie

Fresh fish is brought into Paris daily from ports on the English Channel, 110 miles away. In fact, fish here is likely fresher than in many towns closer to the sea—anything wiggling? This *poissonnerie*, like all such shops, has upgraded to meet Europe-wide hygiene standards.

▶ *Next door, under the awning (get close to see), is a particularly tempting Rue Cler storefront.*

❽ No More Horse Meat

The mosaics and glass set over the doorway advertise horse meat: *Boucherie Chevaline*. While you'll no longer find horse meat here, the classy old storefront survives. Created in the 1930s and signed by the artist, it's a work of art fit for a museum—but it belongs right here, and that's where it will stay.

▶ *A few steps farther, across the street, is...*

❾ A la Mère de Famille Confectionery

This shop has been in the neighborhood for 30 years. The owner sells modern treats but has always kept the traditional candies, too. "The old ladies, they want the same sweets that made them so happy 80 years ago," she says. You can buy chocolate by the piece (about €1 each). You're welcome to assemble a small assortment.

Until a few years ago, the chocolate was dipped and decorated right on the premises. As was the tradition in Rue Cler shops, the merchants resided and produced in the back and sold in the front.

▶ *Next door is the neighborhood's...*

❿ Oldest Building and Charcuterie-Traiteur Jeusselin

Rue Cler's oldest building is at #37—the one with the two garret windows on the roof. It's from the early 1800s, when this street was part of a village near Paris and lined with structures like this.

Occupying the ground floor of this house is Charcuterie-Traiteur Jeusselin—a gourmet deli selling mouthwatering food-to-go. Because Parisian kitchens are so small, locals rely on these places for beautifully prepared side dishes to complete their home-cooked main course.

Charcuteries by definition are pork butchers, specializing in sausage, pâté, and ham. The charcuterie business is fiercely competitive. Jeusselin proudly displays its hard-earned diplomas on its back walls and hard-won awards on the right side of the storefront. Even with such accolades, many charcuteries have had to add *traiteur* services: prepared dishes, pastries, and wines to-go. Jeusselin and its rival **Davoli** (across the street) go *tête à tête*, cooking up *plats du jour*.

Both charcuteries put out their best stuff just before lunch and dinner. If you want a roasted chicken off the spit, pick one up—cooked and hot—at 11:00 or at 17:00, when Parisians buy provisions for that day's meals. Note the system: Order, take your ticket to the cashier to pay, and return with the receipt to pick up your food.

▶ *The ice cream shop next door to Jeusselin,* **Glacier Artisan Martine Lambert,** *serves what many locals consider Paris' best ice cream. A few paces from here you'll find...*

⓫ Café du Marché and More

Café du Marché, on the corner, is *the* place to sit and enjoy the action (see details on page 202). It's Rue Cler's living room, where locals gather before heading home, many staying for a relaxed and affordable dinner. The owner has priced the menu so that residents can afford to dine out on a regular basis, and it works—many patrons eat here five days a week. For a reasonable meal, grab a chair and check the chalk menu listing the *plat du jour*. Notice how the no-indoor-smoking laws have made outdoor seating a huge hit.

Across Rue Cler, the sterile **Aldi grocery store** sells bulk items (*à la* Costco). But because storage space is so limited in Parisian apartments, few locals shop here. The latest shopping trend is to stock up on nonperishables online, pick up produce three times a week, and buy fresh bread daily. Its *moderne* exterior suggests a sneaky bending of Rue Cler's normally rigorous design review for building permits.

▶ *From Café du Marché, hook right and side-trip a couple of doors down Rue du Champ de Mars to visit...*

⓬ L'Epicerie Fine

This fine-foods boutique stands out because of its gentle owners, Pascal and Nathalie. Their mission is to explain to travelers, in fluent English, what the French fuss over food is all about. They'll tempt you with fine gourmet treats, Berthillon ice cream, and generous tastes of caramel, balsamic vinegar, and French and Italian olive oils.

▶ *Return to Rue Cler. The neighborhood bakery on the corner is often marked by a line of people waiting to pick up their daily baguette.*

⓭ Artisan Boulangerie

Since the French Revolution, the government has regulated the cost of a basic baguette. And to call your shop a *boulangerie*, by law you must make the bread on the premises. Locals debate the merits of Paris' many *boulangeries*. Some like their baguette well done, and others

Satisfy your sweet tooth *tout suite*.

Parisians fill tiny homes with *beaucoup* flowers.

prefer it more doughy. It's said that a baker cannot be good at both bread and pastry—at cooking school, they generally major in one or the other. At Artisan Boulangerie, the baker has bucked the trend, demonstrating equal skill at the two specialties, and Rue Cler regulars agree.

▶ *A bit farther along is...*

⑭ Mephisto Shoe Store

Shoe stores are almost as popular as bakeries in this city of footwear-loving fashionistas. (French-made Mephistos are cheaper here than in the US.) In a city where many people don't have cars, good shoes matter. The average Parisian's daily life is active: walking to the Métro, to lunch, to the shops after work, and then home (probably up several flights of stairs).

▶ *Across the street is...*

⑮ Cler Fleurs and Butcher Shop

Almost all Parisians who reside in the city center live in apartments or condos, with no yard. So, Parisians spend small fortunes bringing nature into their homes with plants and fresh flower arrangements. Notice the flower boxes on balconies—you work with what you have.

Pop into the **butcher shop** a few doors down for a graphic peek at the meat Parisians are eating. Check out the chalkboard listing nine cuts of beef (*boeuf*), three kinds of veal (*veau*), four cuts of pork (*porc*), and three cuts of lamb (*agneau*). Traditional butchery is struggling to survive in France, as the younger generation no longer considers it a "desirable" career option, but it continues on Rue Cler.

▶ *Walk to the end of Rue Cler, where it hits a bigger street flooded with cars and buses.*

⑯ City Info Post

An electronic signpost (10 feet up) directs residents to websites for local information—transportation changes, surveys, employment opportunities, community events, and so on. Notice the big glass recycling bin nearby and the see-through garbage sacks. In the 1990s, Paris suffered a rash of trash-can bombings. Perpetrators hid rigged camp-stove canisters in metal garbage cans, which shredded into deadly "shrapnel" when they exploded. City authorities solved this by replacing metal cans with translucent bags.

▶ *Across the busy Avenue de la Motte-Picquet is a tabac.*

⑰ Tabac La Cave à Cigares

Just as the US has liquor stores licensed to sell booze, the only place for people over 18 to buy tobacco legally in France is at a *tabac* (tah-bah) counter. Notice how European laws require a bold warning sign on cigarettes, with graphic, often grotesque photos—about half the size of the package—proclaiming, bluntly, *fumer tue* (smoking kills).

Tabacs serve their neighborhoods as a kind of government cash desk. All sell stamps and some sell public-transit tickets. Like back home, the LOTO is a big deal—and a lucrative way for the government to tax poor and less-educated people.

American smokers may not be able to resist the temptation to pick up a *petit* Habana cigar—your chance to buy a fine Cuban stogie.

▶ *Appropriately, next door you'll find a...*

⑱ Pharmacy

In France, mildly sick people go first to the pharmacist, who has the authority to diagnose and prescribe certain drugs (and more recently, Covid tests and vaccines).

▶ *Your walk is done. If you bought a picnic along this walk, here are two good places to enjoy it: Leaving Rue Cler, turn left on Avenue de la Motte-Picquet for the Army Museum (find the small park after crossing Boulevard de la Tour Maubourg). Or, turn right to reach the Champ de Mars park (and the Eiffel Tower). Or if you're ready to move on, the Ecole Militaire Métro stop is just down Avenue de la Motte-Picquet to the right.*

Versailles Tour

Château de Versailles

Every king's dream, Versailles (vehr-"sigh") was the residence of French monarchs and the cultural heartbeat of Europe for about 100 years. The powerful court of Louis XIV at Versailles set the standard of culture for all of Europe, right up to modern times.

Versailles offers three blockbuster sights. The palace itself—the **Château**—features the lavish, chandeliered rooms of France's kings. The expansive **Gardens** are a landscaped wonderland of statues and fountains. Finally, the **Trianon Palaces and Domaine de Marie-Antoinette** offer a pastoral getaway of small palaces, including Marie's faux-peasant Hamlet.

ORIENTATION

Cost and Reservations: A timed-entry ticket is required to enter the Château. Reserve ahead (no fee) and book your entry time on the Versailles website. You can also purchase Versailles tickets at any Paris TI or at FNAC department stores (small fee). If you have a Paris Museum Pass, see "Using the Paris Museum Pass," later.

Château: €18 (Château only) or €20 Le Passeport ticket (includes Trianon/Domaine; €27 on Garden Spectacle days), both tickets come with audioguide (free on first Sun of the month Nov-March).

Trianon Palaces and Domaine de Marie-Antoinette: €12 (free on the first Sun of the month Nov-March).

Gardens: Free on weekdays April-Oct, except when there are special events (likely on Tue and Fri-Sun in high season—see "Spectacles in the Gardens," later). The Gardens are free daily Nov-March.

Hours: The **Château** is open Tue-Sun 9:00-18:30, Nov-March until 17:30, closed Mon year-round.

The **Trianon Palaces and Domaine de Marie-Antoinette** are open Tue-Sun 12:00-18:30, Nov-March until 17:30, closed Mon year-round, last entry 45 minutes before closing.

The **Gardens** are open daily 8:00-20:30, Nov-March until 18:00.

Information: Use the website to book your entry and check for updates—www.chateauversailles.fr. The free Versailles app includes interactive maps that work without an internet connection. The palace's general contact number is +33 1 30 83 78 00. At the Château, an information office is to the left as you face the palace.

Using the Paris Museum Pass: The Paris Museum Pass covers the most important parts of the complex (Château and Trianon/Domaine); it does not include the Gardens on Spectacle days. To enter using the pass, you must book an entry time ("Palace Ticket"—free) on the Versailles website.

Buying Tickets in Versailles: If you arrive in Versailles without a pass or ticket—and reserved entry time—you may have to wait (sometimes hours or days) to enter the Château. If you have internet access, try the website first. The **Versailles TI** (near the train station) sells tickets and **Get Your Guide** usually has space on its guided tours (€55, across from the train station, under the stone arch at #10). Your last option is the busy **Château ticket-sales office** (to the left as you face the palace).

Crowd-Beating Strategies: In high season, avoid holidays, Sundays, Tuesdays, and Saturdays—in that order—when crowds smother the palace interior. Thursdays and Fridays are best. Everyone must go through two security checkpoints: at the Château's courtyard entry and again at the Château entrance (longest lines 10:00-12:00).

Planning Your Time: Here's how I'd spend the day at Versailles. Leave Paris by 8:00, get in line before the palace opens at 9:00, and follow my self-guided tour of the Château interior. Have lunch. Spend the afternoon touring the Gardens and the Trianon Palaces/Domaine de Marie-Antoinette. To shorten your visit, skip the Trianon/Domaine, which takes 1.5 hours to see, plus a 30-minute walk each way.

Pickpockets: Assume pickpockets are working the tourist crowds.

Getting There: The town of Versailles is 35 minutes southwest of Paris. Take **RER/Train-C** from Gare d'Austerlitz, St. Michel, Musée d'Orsay, Invalides, Pont de l'Alma, or Champ de Mars. Use your Navigo Découverte pass, buy a four-zone all-day Easy pass, or, if paper tickets are still available, buy a round-trip Versailles Rive Gauche/Château ticket from a ticket machine or ticket window (about €7.20 round-trip, credit card or coins, 4/hour). Check the departure board, which will list the next train to "Versailles Rive Gauche/Château" and its track. To reach the Château from the station, follow the flow: Turn right out of the station, then left at the first boulevard, and walk 10 minutes.

To return to Paris from the Versailles Rive Gauche/Château train station, just hop on the next train—all trains departing this station zip back to the city. **Taxis** for the 30-minute ride (without traffic) cost about €65.

Tours: The 1.5-hour English **guided tour** of the Château gives you access to a few extra rooms and lets you skip the security line at the Château entrance (€10). Book in advance on the palace website, or reserve immediately upon arrival at the guided-tours office (in the wing to the left of the Château—but location in flux; ask if you don't see it).

A free and worthwhile **audioguide** is included in your admission. To avoid waiting at the audioguide desk, download (in advance) the free "Palace of Versailles" **app** and listen to the audioguide on your phone.

Or 🎧 download my free Versailles **audio tour.**

Spectacles in the Gardens: The Gardens and fountains at Versailles come alive at selected times (check the website for current hours). The Gardens' fountains are in full squirt during **Les Grandes Eaux Musicales,** with 55 fountains gushing for an hour in the morning and up to two hours in the afternoon; individual fountains run periodically throughout the day; all accompanied by loud classical music (€9.50; April-Oct Sat-Sun 11:00-12:00 & 15:30-17:00, also Tue May-June 11:00-12:00 & 14:30-16:30). On varied weekdays April-Oct, you get the music but no fountains (called **Les Jardins Musicaux,** €8.50).

On Saturday nights in summer, **Les Grandes Eaux Nocturnes** lets you meander past a thousand lights, illuminated groves, and shimmering pools while the fountains play to the sound of the Sun King's music. Your experience ends with fireworks (€29, Sat early June-mid-Sept 20:30-23:00, fireworks at 22:50).

Baggage Check: Free and located just after Château entry security. You must retrieve your items one hour before closing.

Services: WCs are plentiful and well signed in the Château, but fewer and farther between in the Gardens.

Eating: Near the Château entry, the **$ Grand Café d'Orléans** offers good-value self-service meals (great for picnicking in the Gardens). In the Gardens, you'll find several cafés and snack stands with fair prices. One is located near the Latona Fountain (less crowded) and others are clustered at the Grand Canal.

In the Versailles town center, the best choices are along traffic-free Rue de Satory or on the lively Place du Marché.

Starring: Luxurious palaces, endless gardens, Louis XIV, Marie-Antoinette, and the *ancien régime.*

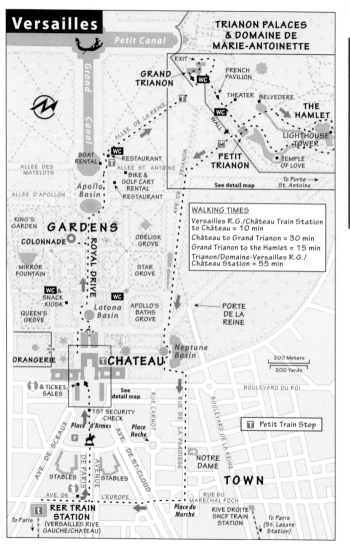

THE TOUR BEGINS

▶ *On this self-guided tour, we'll see the Château, the landscaped Gardens in the "backyard," and the Trianon Palaces and Domaine de Marie-Antoinette, located at the far end of the Gardens. Stand in the huge courtyard and face the palace. The entrance to the Château is marked Entrance A (where the line usually is).*

Original Château and Courtyard

The section of the palace with the clock is the original château, once a small hunting lodge where little Louis XIV spent his happiest boyhood years. Naturally, the Sun King's private bedroom (the three arched windows beneath the clock) faced the rising sun. The palace and grounds are laid out on an east-west axis.

Once king, Louis XIV expanded the lodge by attaching wings, creating the present U-shape. Later, the long north and south wings were built. The total cost of the project has been estimated at half of France's entire GNP for one year.

Think how busy this courtyard must have been 300 years ago. As many as 5,000 nobles were here at any one time, each with an entourage. Riding in sedan-chair taxis, they'd buzz from games to parties to amorous rendezvous. Servants ran about delivering secret messages and roast legs of lamb. Horse-drawn carriages arrived at the fancy gate with their finely dressed passengers, having driven up the broad boulevard that ran directly from Paris. Then, as now, there were hordes of tourists, pickpockets, palace workers, and vendors selling wind-up children's toys.

▶ *As you enter the Château, you'll find an information desk (get a map)*

Entrance A—security checkpoint

Original Château and courtyard

We Three Kings

Versailles was the residence of the king and the seat of France's government for a hundred years. With 18 million people united under one king (England had only 5.5 million), a booming economy, and a powerful military, France was Europe's number-one power, and Versailles was its cultural heartbeat. Everyone learned French. French taste in clothes, hairstyles, table manners, theater, music, art, and kissing spread across the Continent.

Three kings lived in Versailles during its century of glory:

Louis XIV (reigned 1643-1715), Europe's greatest king, built Versailles and established French dominance.

Louis XV (r. 1715-1774) was his great-grandson. (Louis XIV reigned for 72 years, outliving several heirs.) Louis XV carried on the tradition and policies, but without the Sun King's flair. France's power abroad was weakening, and there were rumblings of rebellion from within.

Louis XVI (r. 1774-1792), a shy, meek bookworm, inherited a nation in crisis. He married a sweet girl from the Austrian royal family, Marie-Antoinette, and together they retreated into the idyllic gardens of Versailles while revolutionary fires smoldered. Each had their final day on Paris' Place de la Concorde, thanks to the brutally efficient guillotine.

and bag check. Follow the crowds directly across the courtyard, where you'll go back inside. If you haven't already downloaded the official Versailles app, line up here for your free (and worth-the-wait) audioguide. Now make your way to the start of our tour.

Just follow the flow through a number of rooms. Climb the stairs. You'll eventually reach a palatial golden-brown room, with a doorway that overlooks the Royal Chapel.

Royal Chapel

Dut-dutta-dah! Every morning at 10:00, the organist and musicians struck up the music, these big golden doors opened, and Louis XIV and his family stepped onto the balcony to attend Mass. While Louis looked down on the golden altar, the lowly nobles on the ground floor knelt with their backs to the altar and looked up—worshipping Louis worshipping God. Important religious ceremonies took place here, including the marriage of young Louis XVI to Marie-Antoinette.

The Royal Chapel, where Louis VIX worshipped and allowed himself to be worshipped

In the vast pagan "temple" that is Versailles—built to glorify one man, Louis XIV—this Royal Chapel is a paltry tip of the hat to that "other" god...the Christian one.

▶ *Enter the next room, an even more sumptuous space with a fireplace and a colorful painting on the ceiling.*

Hercules Drawing Room

Pleasure ruled. The main suppers, balls, and receptions were held in this room. Picture elegant partygoers in fine silks, wigs, rouge, lipstick, and fake moles (and that's just the men) as they dance to the strains of a string quartet.

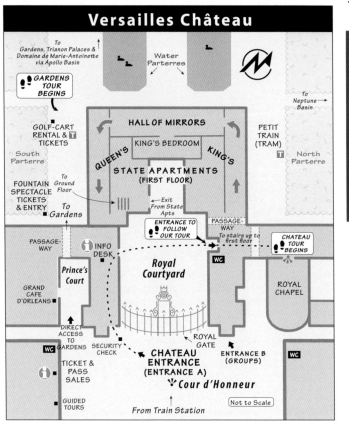

Versailles Château

To
Gardens, Trianon Palaces &
Domaine de Marie-Antoinette
via Apollo Basin

Water
Parterres

**GARDENS
TOUR
BEGINS**

GOLF-CART
RENTAL & 🚻
TICKETS

To
Neptune →
Basin

HALL OF MIRRORS

KING'S BEDROOM

PETIT
TRAIN
(TRAM)

🚇

South
Parterre

QUEEN'S

KING'S

North
Parterre

STATE APARTMENTS
(FIRST FLOOR)

FOUNTAIN
SPECTACLE
TICKETS
& ENTRY

To
Ground
Floor

■ To
Gardens

← Exit
From State
Apts

**ENTRANCE TO
FOLLOW
OUR TOUR**

PASSAGE-
WAY

To stairs up to
first floor

**CHATEAU
TOUR
BEGINS**

PASSAGE-
WAY

ℹ **INFO
DESK**

WC

**Prince's
Court**

**Royal
Courtyard**

**ROYAL
CHAPEL**

GRAND
CAFE
D'ORLEANS ■

DIRECT
ACCESS
TO
GARDENS

WC

SECURITY
CHECK

ROYAL
GATE

ℹ

TICKET
& PASS
SALES

**CHATEAU
ENTRANCE
(ENTRANCE A)**

ENTRANCE B
(GROUPS)

WC

■ GUIDED
TOURS

🔽 *Cour d'Honneur*

From Train Station

Not to Scale

On the wall opposite the fireplace is an appropriate painting showing Christ in the middle of a Venetian party. The work by
Paolo Veronese was one of Louis XIV's favorites, so the king had the
room decorated around it. Stand by the fireplace for the full effect:
The room's columns, arches, and frieze match the height and style of
Veronese's painted architecture, which makes the painting an exten-
sion of the room.

Louis XIV—The Sun King

Louis XIV was a true Renaissance Man, a century after the Renaissance: athletic, good-looking, a musician, dancer, horseman, statesman, patron of the arts, and lover. He was a good listener who could put even commoners at ease.

Louis XIV, age 63, by Hyacinthe Rigaud

Louis had grown up in the previous royal residence—the Louvre in Paris. When he became king, he moved the government to the forests of Versailles, where he'd hunted as a kid. There, he could concentrate power around himself. He invited France's nobles—who in other countries were the center of power—to live at Versailles. They became virtual slaves of pleasure, dependent on Louis' generosity, while he made the important decisions.

Louis XIV called himself the Sun King because he gave life and warmth to all he touched. He was also thought of as Apollo, the Greek god of the sun. Versailles became the personal temple of this god on earth, decorated with statues and symbols of Apollo, the sun, and Louis XIV himself.

For more than 70 years he was the perfect embodiment of the absolute monarch. He summed it up best himself with his famous rhyme—*"L'état, c'est moi!"* (lay-tah say-mwah): "The state, that's me!"

The ceiling painting creates the effect of a sunroof opening up to heaven. Hercules (with his club) hurries up to heaven on a chariot, late for his wedding to the king of the gods' daughter. The scene echoes real life—Louis XIV built the room for his own daughter's wedding reception.

▶ *From here on it's a one-way tour—getting lost is not allowed. Follow the crowds into the **King's Wing** starting with a small green room with a goddess in pink on the ceiling. The names of the rooms generally come from the paintings on the ceilings.*

Hercules among the gods

Venus Room ceiling painting

Salon of Abundance

If the party in the Hercules Room got too intense, you could always step in here for some refreshments. Silver trays were loaded with liqueurs, exotic stimulants (coffee), juice, chocolates, and, on really special occasions, three-bean salad.

Louis was a gracious host who enjoyed letting his hair down at night. If he took a liking to you, he might sneak you through those doors there (in the middle of the wall) and into his own private study, where he'd show off his collection of dishes, medals, jewels, or...the *Mona Lisa,* which hung on his wall.

Venus Room

Love ruled at Versailles. In this room, couples would cavort beneath the goddess of love floating on the ceiling. Venus sends down a canopy of flowery garlands to ensnare mortals in delicious amour. Notice how in the paintings at both ends of the room, the painted columns match the real ones, extending this grand room into mythical courtyards.

Don't let the statue of a confident Louis XIV as a Roman emperor fool you. He started out as a poor little rich kid with a chip on his shoulder. The French *parlements* treated little Louis and his mother as virtual prisoners in their home, the Royal Palace in Paris (today's Louvre). There they eked by with bland meals, hand-me-down leotards, and pointed shoes. After Louis XIV attained power and wealth, he made Versailles a pleasure palace—his way of saying, "Living well is the best revenge."

Venus Room—Louis XIV as emperor

Mercury Room—the king's official bedroom

Diana Room

Here in the billiards room, Louis and his men played on a table that stood in the center of the room, while ladies sat surrounding them on Persian-carpet cushions, and music wafted in from next door. Louis was a good pool player, a sore loser, and a king—thus, he rarely lost.

The famous bust of Louis by Giovanni Lorenzo Bernini (in the center) shows a handsome, dashing, 27-year-old playboy-king. His gaze is steady amid his windblown cloak and hair. Young Louis loved life. He hunted animals by day (notice Diana the Huntress, with her bow, on the ceiling) and chased beautiful women at night.

Games were actually an important part of Louis' political strategy, known as "the domestication of the nobility." By distracting the nobles with the pleasures of courtly life, he was free to run the government his way. The biggest distraction was gambling, usually a card game similar to blackjack. Louis lent money to the losers, making them even more indebted to him. The good life was an addiction, and Louis kept the medicine cabinet well-stocked.

Mars Room

Also known as the Guard Room (as it was the room for Louis' Swiss bodyguards), this red room is decorated with a military flair. On the ceiling is Mars, the Greek god of war, in a chariot pulled by wolves. Most of the furniture we see today is not original, but is from the same period.

Mercury Room

Louis' life was a work of art, and Versailles was the display case. Everything he did was a public event designed to show his subjects how it should be done. This room may have served as Louis' official (not actual) bedroom, where the Sun King would ritually rise each morning to warm his subjects.

From a canopied bed (like this 18th-century one), Louis would get up, dress, and take a seat for morning prayer. Meanwhile, the nobles would stand and watch, in awe of his piety, nobility, and clean socks. At breakfast, they murmured with delight as he deftly decapitated his boiled egg with a knife. And when Louis went to bed at night, the dukes and barons would fight over who got to hold the candle while he slipped into his royal jammies.

Apollo Room

This was the grand throne room. Louis held court from a 10-foot-tall, silver-and-gold canopied throne on a raised platform placed in the center of the room.

Everything in here reminds us of Louis XIV's glory. On the ceiling, the sun god Apollo (representing Louis) drives his chariot, dragging the sun across the heavens to warm the four corners of the world—including good ol' America, symbolized by a Native American maiden with a crocodile.

The famous portrait by Hyacinthe Rigaud over the fireplace gives a more human look at Louis XIV, age 63. He's shown in a dancer's pose, displaying the legs that made him one of the all-time dancing fools of kingery. At night, they often held parties in this room, actually dancing around the throne.

Louis had more than 300 wigs like this one. The fashion sprouted all over Europe, even spreading to the American colonies.

Louis XIV may have been treated like a god, but his subjects adored him as a symbol of everything a man could be, the fullest expression of the Renaissance Man.

▶ *Continue into the final room of the King's Wing.*

War Room

"Louis Quatorze was addicted to wars," and the room depicts his victories—in marble, gilding, stucco, and paint. On the ceiling, Lady France hurls thunderbolts down to defeat her foes. The relief on the wall shows Louis XIV on horseback, triumphing over his fallen

The Hall of Mirrors—a grand ballroom of chandeliers, mirrored walls, and staggering views

enemies. But Louis's greatest triumph may be the next room, the one that everybody wrote home about.

Hall of Mirrors

No one had ever seen anything like this hall when it was opened. Mirrors were still a great luxury at the time, and the number and size of these monsters was astounding. The hall is nearly 250 feet long. There are 17 arched mirrors, matched by 17 windows letting in that breathtaking view of the Gardens. Lining the hall are 24 gilded candelabra, eight busts of Roman emperors, and eight classical-style statues (seven of them ancient). The ceiling shows Louis in the central panel doing what he did best—triumphing.

Imagine this place lit by the flames of thousands of candles, filled with ambassadors, nobles, and guests dressed in silks and powdered wigs. At the far end of the room sits the king, on the canopied throne moved in temporarily from the Apollo Room. Servants glide by with silver trays of hors d'oeuvres, and an orchestra fuels the festivities. The mirrors reflect an age when beautiful people loved to look at themselves. It was no longer a sin to be proud of good looks and fine clothes, or to enjoy the good things in life: laughing, dancing, eating, drinking, flirting, and watching the sun set into the distant canal.

From the center of the hall you can fully appreciate the epic scale of Versailles. The huge palace (by architect Louis Le Vau), the fantasy interior (by Charles Le Brun), and the endless gardens (by André Le Nôtre) made Versailles *le* best. In 1919, Germany and the Allies signed the Treaty of Versailles, ending World War I (and, some say, starting World War II) right here, in the Hall of Mirrors.

▶ *Backtrack a few stops to find the door that leads into the heart of the palace, to the...*

King's Bedroom and Council Rooms

Pass through a first large room to find Louis XIV's bedroom. It's elaborately decorated with an impressive bed and balustrade, and the decor changed with the season. Find an uncovered window and notice how this small room is at the exact center of the immense horseshoe-shaped building, overlooking the main courtyard and—naturally—facing the rising sun in the east. It symbolized the exact center of power in France. Imagine the humiliation on that day in 1789 when Louis' great-great-great-grandson, Louis XVI, was forced to stand here and acknowledge the angry crowds that filled the square demanding the end of the divine monarchy.

▶ *Return to the Hall of Mirrors, and continue to the end, being sure to enjoy views of the garden. Enter the...*

Peace Room

By the end of the Sun King's long life, he was tired of fighting. In this sequel to the War Room, peace is granted to Germany, Holland, and

King's bedroom—heart of the palace

View down the Royal Drive—eight-mile axis

Queen's bedroom for royal rendezvous

Coronation room, Queen's Wing

Spain as cupids play with the discarded cannons, and swords are transformed into violins. Louis XIV advised his great-grandson to "be a peaceful king," and it appears he was listening. The oval painting above the fireplace shows 19-year-old Louis XV bestowing an olive branch on Europe.

▸ *The Peace Room marks the beginning of the* **Queen's Wing,** *a suite of rooms where France's queens lived, slept, ate, and entertained. Enter the first room.*

Queen's Bedchamber

It was here that the queen rendezvoused with her husband. Two queens died here, and this is where 19 princes were born. This room looks just like it did in the days of the last queen, Marie-Antoinette. That's her bust over the fireplace, and the double eagle of her native Austria in two of the corners. The big mahogany chest to the left of the bed held her jewels. The large canopied bed is a reconstruction. The bed, chair, and wall coverings switched with the seasons. This was the cheery summer pattern.

Salon of the Nobles

Here, in this mint green room, the wife of Louis XV and her circle of friends held discussions ranging from politics to gossip, food to literature, fashion to philosophy. All three of Versailles' rulers considered themselves enlightened monarchs who promoted the arts and new ideas. Ironically, these discussions planted the seeds of liberal thought that would grow into the Revolution.

Queen's Antechamber

The royal family dined publicly in this room (also called the Grand Couvert). A typical dinner consisted of four soups, two whole birds stuffed with truffles, mutton, ham slices, fruit, pastries, compotes, and preserves. You may see a painting of luxury-loving, "let-them-eat-cake" Marie-Antoinette. The portrait is a public-relations attempt to soften her image by showing her with three of her children.

Queen's Guard Room

On October 5, 1789, a mob of revolutionaries—perhaps appalled by their queen's taste in wallpaper—stormed the palace. They burst into this room, where Marie-Antoinette was hiding; overcame her bodyguards; and dragged her off along with her husband. The enraged peasants then proceeded to ransack the place as revenge for the years of poverty and oppression they'd suffered. (The stripped palace was refurnished a decade later and eventually turned into a national museum.)

Coronation Room

No sooner did the French throw out a king than they got an emperor. This room captures the glory of the Napoleonic years, when Napoleon Bonaparte conquered most of Europe. In the huge canvas, we see him crowning himself emperor of a new, revived "Roman" Empire. (The original by Jacques-Louis David now hangs in the Louvre.)

Turn and face the windows to see the portrait of a dashing, young, charismatic Napoleon in 1796. Compare the young Napoleon with the adjacent portrait from 10 years later—looking less like a revolutionary and more like a Louis.

▶ *This ends our tour of the Château. From here, head down the stairs and consider a break in the **Salon de Thé Angelina.** Continuing downstairs, exit the palace, and turn right into the Gardens (les Jardins), located behind the Château.*

THE GARDENS

Louis XIV was a divine-right ruler. One way he proved it was by controlling nature like a god. These lavish grounds—elaborately planned, pruned, and decorated—showed everyone that Louis was in total command.

The Gardens are vast. For some, a stroll through the landscaped shrubs around the Château and quick view down the Royal Drive is plenty. But it's worth the 10-minute walk down the Royal Drive to the Apollo Basin and back (even if you don't continue further to the Trianon/Domaine).

▶ *Entering the Gardens, make your way into the king's spacious backyard until you reach the top step of a staircase overlooking the Gardens. Face away from the palace and take in the jaw-dropping...*

View Down the Royal Drive

This, to me, is the most stunning spot in all of Versailles. With the palace behind you, it seems as if the grounds stretch out forever. Versailles was laid out along an eight-mile axis that included the grounds, the palace, and the town of Versailles itself, one of the first instances of urban planning since Roman times and a model for future capitals, such as Washington, DC, and Brasilia.

Looking down the Royal Drive, you see the round Apollo fountain in the distance. Just beyond that is the Grand Canal. The groves on either side of the Royal Drive were planted with trees from all over, laid out in an elaborate grid, and dotted with statues and fountains. Of the original 1,500 fountains, 300 remain.

▶ *Stroll down the steps to get a good look at the frogs and lizards that fill the round...*

Latona Basin

This round fountain tells the story of the birth of Apollo and his sister, Diana. On top of the fountain are Apollo and Diana as little kids with their mother, Latona (they're facing toward the Apollo fountain). Latona, an unwed mother, was insulted by the local peasants, so Zeus swooped down and turned them into frogs and lizards.

▶ *As you walk, you'll pass by "ancient" statues done by 17th-century French sculptors. Find the Colonnade, hidden in the woods on the left*

The Latona Basin fountain—symbolic of Louis the XIV's early childhood

Getting Around the Gardens

On Foot: It's a 45- to 60-minute walk (plus sightseeing) from the palace, down to the Grand Canal, past the two Trianon palaces, to the Hamlet at the far end of Domaine de Marie-Antoinette.

By Bike: There's a bike-rental station by the Grand Canal (about €9/hour or €20/half-day, daily 10:00-18:30). You can't take your bike inside the grounds of the Trianon/Domaine, but you can park it nearby.

By Petit Train: The slow-moving tram leaves from behind the Château and makes a one-way loop, stopping at the Grand Trianon and Petit Trianon, then the Grand Canal before returning to the Château (€8.50 round-trip, €4.60 one-way, 2-4/hour, Tue-Sun 11:30-19:00, Mon 11:00-17:00, shorter hours in winter).

By Golf Cart: These make for a fun drive through the Gardens, but you can't take them inside the Trianon/Domaine, and they only go along a prescribed route (€38/hour, €9/15 minutes after that, 4-person limit per cart, rental stations by the canal and behind the Château—near the Gardens entrance).

side of the Royal Drive, about three-fourths of the way to the Apollo Basin.

Colonnade

Versailles had no prestigious ancient ruins, so the king built his own. This prefab Roman ruin is a 100-foot circle of 64 red-marble columns supporting pure white arches. Nobles would picnic in the shade to the tunes of a string quartet and pretend that they were the enlightened citizens of the ancient world.

Apollo Basin

The fountains of Versailles were once its most famous attraction. This one was the centerpiece, showing the sun god—Louis XIV—in his sunny chariot as he starts his journey across the sky. The horses are half-submerged, giving the impression, when the fountains play, of the sun rising out of the mists of dawn.

All the fountains are gravity-powered. Underground streams

The Apollo Basin: The sun god rises from the mist on days when the fountains play.

(pumped into Versailles by Seine River pressure) feed into smaller pipes at the fountains, which shoot the water high into the air.

Looking back at the palace from here, realize that the distance you just walked is only a fraction of this vast complex of buildings, gardens, and waterways. Be glad you don't have to mow the lawn.

Grand Canal

In an era before virtual reality, this was the next best thing to an actual trip to Venice. Couples in gondolas would pole along the waters accompanied by barges with orchestras playing *"O Sole Mio."* The canal is one mile from end to end.

▶ *Next stop, the Trianon Palaces and Domaine de Marie-Antoinette, a walled-off part of the Gardens accessible only with a ticket.*

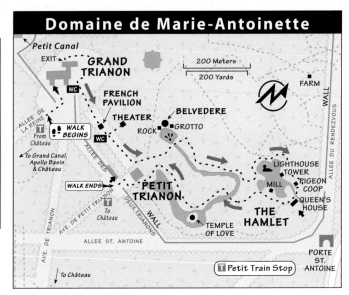

TRIANON PALACES AND DOMAINE DE MARIE-ANTOINETTE

Versailles began as an escape from the pressures of kingship. But in a short time, the Château became as busy as Paris ever was. Louis XIV needed an escape from his escape, so he built a smaller palace out in the boonies. Later, his successors retreated still farther from the Château and French political life, ignoring the real world that was crumbling all around them. They expanded the Trianon area, building a fantasy world of palaces, ponds, pavilions, and pleasure gardens—the enclosure called Marie-Antoinette's Domaine.

Grand Trianon

Delicate, pink, and set amid gardens, the Grand Trianon was the perfect summer getaway. This was the king's private residence away from the main palace. Louis XIV usually spent a couple of nights a week here, near the tiny peasant village of Trianon (hence the name).

Louis XIV's bedroom: Wake up with the king.

Grand Trianon—gardens in back

Inside, the rooms are a complex overlay of furnishings from many different kings, dauphins, and nobles who lived here over the centuries. Louis XIV alone had three different bedrooms. Concentrate on the illustrious time of Louis XIV (1688-1715) and Napoleon Bonaparte (1810-1814).

The spacious **Mirrors Salon** (Room 2) has the original white walls and mirrors of Louis XIV, and the Empire-style furniture of Napoleon (unornamented, high-polished wood, with classical motifs). In the **Bedroom of the Empress** (Room 3), imagine waking up in this big bed with your lover, throwing back the curtain, and looking out the windows at the gardens. Exit into the open-air **colonnade** (Peristyle) that connects the two wings. Originally, this pink-columned passageway had windows, an enormously expensive luxury that allowed visitors to enjoy the gardens even in bad weather.

The **Emperor's Family Drawing Room** (Room 7) was a theater for Louis XIV, a game room for Louis XV, and Napoleon's family room. After Napoleon was defeated and France's royalty returned, King Louis-Philippe I lived here. Walk through a series of rooms until you reach the **Malachite Room** (Room 11). This was Napoleon's living room. You'll see the impressive green basin, vases, and candelabras made of Russian malachite given to Napoleon by Czar Alexander I.

▶ *Our next stop is the French Pavilion. To get there, walk clockwise around the perimeter of the Grand Trianon. Make it a tight, 180-degree loop, hugging the palace on your right, and follow signs to the* Petit Trianon. *A path leads across a footbridge. Directly ahead, you'll see the...*

French Pavilion—one of many hidden gems

French Pavilion

This small, cream-colored building (generally closed) with rooms fanning out from the center has big French doors to let in a cool breeze. Here Marie-Antoinette spent summer evenings with family and a few friends, listening to music or playing parlor games, exploring all avenues of *la douceur de vivre*, the sweetness of living.

▶ *Up ahead is the large, cube-shaped Petit Trianon palace. But midway there, turn left, where you can peek into...*

Marie-Antoinette's Theater

Marie-Antoinette was an aspiring performer. In this plush, 100-seat dollhouse theater, the queen and her friends acted out plays for a select audience.

▶ *Just before reaching the Petit Trianon, find the nearby...*

Belvedere—tiny palace above a pond

Belvedere, Rock, and Grotto

The octagonal Belvedere palace is as much windows as it is walls. When the doors were open, it could serve as a gazebo for musicians, serenading nobles in this man-made alpine setting. To the left of the Belvedere is the "Rock," a fake mountain that pours water into the pond. To the right of the Belvedere (you'll have to find it) is the secret Grotto.

▶ *Facing the Belvedere, turn right (east), following the pond's meandering stream. Continue until you spy a round, fanciful tower and a smattering of rustic, half-timbered buildings. Head there to find the Hansel-and-Gretel-like...*

Hamlet

Marie-Antoinette longed for the simple life of a peasant—not the hard labor of real peasants, who sweated and starved around her, but the fairy-tale world of simple country pleasures. The main building is the Queen's House—two buildings connected by a wooden skywalk. Like any typical peasant farmhouse, it had a billiard room, library, elegant

The Hamlet—a faux peasant village

Temple of Love—perfect for a rendezvous

dining hall, and two living rooms. This was an actual working farm with a dairy (walk past the lighthouse tower), a water mill, a pigeon coop, and domestic animals. Beyond the lighthouse tower, you'll see where the queen's servants kept cows, goats, chickens, and ducks.

▶ *Head back toward the Petit Trianon. Along the way, you'll see the white dome of the...*

Temple of Love

A circle of 12 marble Corinthian columns supports a dome, decorating a path where lovers could stroll. It's a delightful monument to a society where the rich could afford that ultimate luxury: romantic love.

Petit Trianon

Louis XV built the Petit Trianon as a place to rendezvous with his mistress Madame de Pompadour. He later gave it to his next mistress, Countess du Barry. After the crown passed to Louis XVI, it became the principal residence of Marie-Antoinette, who was uncomfortable with the court intrigue in the big Château. As you tour the Petit Trianon, you'll see portraits and historical traces of this intriguing cast of characters.

As you exit, don't miss her small **bathroom,** with a state-of-the-art hole in a wooden plank.

Marie-Antoinette made the Petit Trianon her home base. On the lawn outside, she installed a carousel. Despite her bad reputation with the public, Marie-Antoinette was a sweet girl from Vienna who never quite fit in with the fast, sophisticated crowd at Versailles. At the Petit Trianon, she could get away and re-create the charming home life that she remembered from her childhood. Here she played, while in the

Petit Trianon—four-faced palace

cafés of faraway Paris, revolutionaries plotted the end of the *ancien régime.*

▶ The main **Château** is a 30-minute walk straight out the exit to the southeast (plus another 10 minutes to reach the train station). Or you can ride the petit train from here back to the Château. It leaves from just outside the wall at the Petit Trianon. For a slightly shorter walk back to the train station by way of **downtown Versailles,** follow the "Versailles" map earlier in this chapter.

Sights

Paris is blessed with world-class museums (the Louvre, the Orsay) and monuments (Eiffel Tower, Arc de Triomphe) as well as grand boulevards, historical churches, and avant-garde architecture—more than anyone could see in a single visit. Let this guide to the City of Light's top sights illuminate your trip.

The following sights are clustered into walkable neighborhoods for more efficient sightseeing. When you see a 📖 in a listing, it means the sight is described in greater detail in one of the self-guided walks or tours in this book. There you'll also find crucial details on how to avoid lines, save money, and get a bite to eat nearby. A 🎧 means the walk or tour is available as a free audio tour (see page 12).

ADVANCE TICKETS AND SIGHTSEEING PASSES

Virtually all sights of any importance in Paris sell tickets online for no additional fee. At a few key sights, you can't get in without a timed-entry ticket bought in advance: the **Louvre,** the **Orangerie, Sainte-Chapelle,** and **Versailles.** Although advance tickets are not technically required for the **Eiffel Tower, Catacombs,** and **Conciergerie,** I recommend booking ahead.

Even where advance tickets are not required, buying ahead lets you avoid the long ticket-buying lines (though you'll still likely have to wait in a security line). Better yet, combine this strategy with a **Paris Museum Pass** (described below), and you'll save both time and money.

Booking Tickets in Advance

Buy your ticket online, save the digital ticket to your phone (or keep it in your email), and bypass any ticket-buying lines when you get to the sight.

Always book directly on the sight's official website. The process can be cumbersome, as you may need to create an account and go through several tedious steps. If you have a Paris Museum Pass and are reserving a sight covered by the pass, look for the pass holder option (sometimes called *free ticket option*), which lets you book an entry time for free. You'll need to input your Museum Pass number.

Once you've booked, you'll receive an email—usually with a QR code—that acts as your digital ticket. When you arrive at the sight, look for a line marked "ticket holders" (*avec billet*).

Paris Museum Pass

Most of Paris' major sights are covered by the Paris Museum Pass, including the Louvre, Orsay, Sainte-Chapelle, and Versailles. Key sights that are *not* covered are the Eiffel Tower, Montparnasse Tower, Marmottan Museum, Opéra Garnier, and Catacombs. The pass admits you to sights in two, four, or six consecutive days—saving you money if you visit several included sights (2 days-€52, 4 days-€66, 6 days-€78; no youth or senior discounts). The pass pays for itself with four key admissions in two days (for example, the Louvre, Orsay, Sainte-Chapelle, and Rodin Museum).

Pertinent details about the pass are outlined here. For more info, and to purchase the pass online, visit www.parismuseumpass.com. If you wait to buy a pass until you arrive in Paris, it is sold at participating museums, monuments, TIs (small fee added), and some souvenir stores near major sights. Don't buy the pass at a major museum (such as the Louvre), where the supply can be spotty and lines long.

At covered sights where reservations are required—such as the Louvre—even with the pass you must book a free timed entry online in advance. Plan carefully to make the most of your pass. Start using it only when you're ready to tackle the covered sights on consecutive days. Make sure the sights you want to visit will be open when you want to go (many museums are closed Mon or Tue).

Last-Ditch Ticket Tips

If you can't get an online reservation for the date you want, you can buy skip-the-line *"coupe-file"* tickets (pronounced "koop feel") through third party vendors—usually for a high fee. You'll find *coupe-file* tickets at TIs, FNAC department stores, and travel-service companies such as Paris Webservices and Fat Tire Tours.

HISTORIC CORE OF PARIS

▲▲▲Notre-Dame Cathedral
(Cathédrale Notre-Dame de Paris)

This 850-year-old cathedral, packed with history, is recovering from a devastating fire in 2019. While the interior and some of the surrounding areas will be closed for several years, you can still appreciate its monumental exterior.

📖 See the Historic Paris Walk chapter.

▲Paris Archaeological Crypt

Visit Roman ruins, trace the street plan of the medieval village, and see diagrams of how early Paris grew. The ruins are a confusing mix of foundations from every time period—the city's oldest rampart, a medieval road, or a Roman building with a heated floor—but interesting multimedia displays help sort them out.

▶ *€8, covered by Museum Pass, Tue-Sun 10:00-18:00, closed Mon, good audioguide-€5, enter 100 yards in front of cathedral, +33 1 55 42 50 10, www.crypte.paris.fr.*

Sainte-Chapelle's soaring stained-glass windows

▲Deportation Memorial (Mémorial de la Déportation)

Climb down the steps to witness a sober remembrance of the 200,000 French victims of the Nazi concentration camps.

📖 See the Historic Paris Walk chapter.

▲▲▲Sainte-Chapelle

Europe's best stained glass—and that's saying something!—makes this small Gothic church glow.

📖 See the Historic Paris Walk chapter.

▲Conciergerie

Marie-Antoinette and thousands of others were imprisoned here on their way to the guillotine. Exhibits with good English descriptions trace the history of the building and give some insight into prison life.

▶ *€11.50 for timed-entry ticket, €18.50 combo-ticket with Sainte-Chapelle, covered by Museum Pass, daily 9:30-18:00, multimedia guide-€5, 2 Boulevard du Palais, Mo: Cité, +33 1 53 40 60 80, www. paris-conciergerie.fr.*

📖 See the Historic Paris Walk chapter.

▲▲**Riverside Promenades and Paris Plages**

Paris has turned sections of the Seine's embankment into traffic-free areas for strolling, biking, having fun with the kids, dining, or simply dangling one's feet over the water. One section runs along the Left Bank between Pont de l'Alma (near the Eiffel Tower) and the Orsay, and another runs along the Right Bank between the Louvre and Place de la Bastille. The **Paris Plages** (beaches) add lots of activities each summer with a string of faux beaches assembled along a one-mile stretch of the Right Bank.

▶ *Free, promenades always open, Plages run mid-July-mid-Aug.*

MAJOR MUSEUMS NEIGHBORHOOD

▲▲▲**Louvre (Musée du Louvre)**

Europe's oldest, biggest, greatest, and second-most-crowded museum (after the Vatican) is home to *Mona Lisa, Venus de Milo,* and other masterpieces of Western Civilization.

   📖 See the Louvre Tour chapter.

▲▲▲**Orsay Museum (Musée d'Orsay)**

Europe's greatest collection of Impressionist works, Post-Impressionists, and more.

   📖 See the Orsay Museum Tour chapter.

▲▲**Orangerie Museum (Musée de l'Orangerie)**

The Orangerie (oh-rahn-zhuh-ree) is a little bijou of select works by Claude Monet and his contemporaries. Start with the museum's claim to fame: Monet's *Water Lilies.* These eight mammoth, curved panels immerse you in Monet's garden. Working at his home in Giverny, Monet built a special studio with skylights and wheeled easels to accommodate the canvases. Some call this the first "art installation"—art displayed in a space specially designed to enhance the viewer's experience. We're looking at the pond in his garden at Giverny—dotted with water lilies, surrounded by foliage, and dappled with the reflections of the sky, clouds, and trees on the surface.

    Downstairs you'll see artists that bridge the Impressionist and Modernist worlds—Utrillo, Cézanne, Renoir, Matisse, and Picasso.

Major Museums Neighborhood

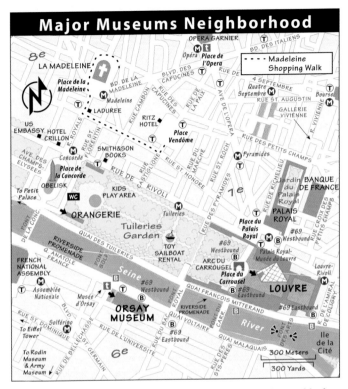

Together they provide a snapshot of what was hot in the world of art collecting, circa 1920.

▶ €12.50 for timed-entry ticket—reserve online, free on first Sun of the month, €18 combo-ticket with Orsay Museum, ask about combo-ticket with Monet's garden and house at Giverny, covered by Museum Pass; Wed-Mon 9:00-18:00, closed Tue; audioguide-€5, English guided tours available-€6, in Tuileries Garden near Place de la Concorde (Mo: Concorde), +33 1 44 77 80 07, www.musee-orangerie.fr.

Orangerie—Monet's eight monumental canvases immerse you in his garden world of Giverny.

EIFFEL TOWER AND NEARBY

▲▲▲Eiffel Tower (La Tour Eiffel)

The 1,063-foot tower was built as a tourist attraction, and it's still the must-see sight in Paris.

    📖 See the Eiffel Tower Tour chapter.

▲Paris Sewer Museum (Les Egouts de Paris)

Discover what happens after you flush. This quick, interesting, and slightly stinky visit takes you along a few hundred yards of water tunnels in the world's first underground sewer system. Trace the sewer's evolution: from Roman times to medieval (washed straight into the river), to Victor Hugo's fictional hero Jean Valjean (who hid here in *Les Misérables*), to today's 1,500 miles of tunnels carrying 317 million gallons of water daily. The loaner booklet, map, and audioguide in English (if available) are essential.

▶ *€9, covered by Museum Pass; Tue-Sun 10:00-17:00, closed Mon, last entry one hour before closing; audioguide-€3, located where Pont de l'Alma greets the Left Bank—on the right side of the bridge as you face*

Eiffel Tower & Nearby

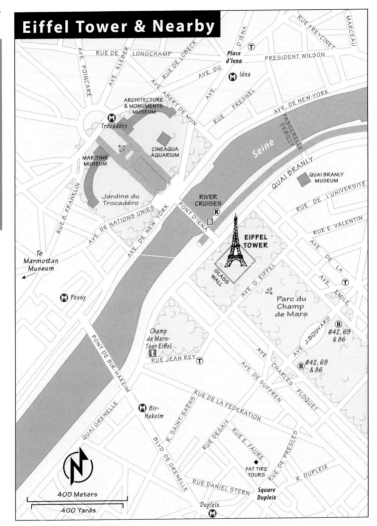

RUE FREYCINET

MARCEAU

RUE KLEBER LONGCHAMP

RUE DE LÜBECK

D'IENA

Place d'lena

PRESIDENT WILSON

AVE. POINCARÉ

AVE. DU

AVE. KLEBER

RUE ABERT DE MUN

Iéna

AVE.

RUE FRESNEL

AVE. DE NEW-YORK

ARCHITECTURE & MONUMENTS MUSEUM

Trocadéro

CINEAQUA AQUARIUM

Seine

PASSERELLE DEBILLY

QUAI BRANLY

QUAI BRANLY MUSEUM

MARITIME MUSEUM

RUE DE L'UNIVERSITÉ

RUE B. FRANKLIN

Jardins du Trocadéro

AVE. DE NATIONS UNIES

RIVER CRUISES

PONT D'IÉNA

RUE E. VALENTIN

EIFFEL TOWER

To Marmottan Museum

AVE. DE NEW YORK

GLASS WALL

AVE. DE LA

Passy

AVE. G. EIFFEL

Parc du Champ de Mars

AVE. EMILE

PONT DE BIR-HAKEIM

Champ de Mars-Tour Eiffel

AVE. J-BOUVARD

#42, 69 & 86

RUE JEAN REY

AVE. CHARLES FLOQUET

#42, 69 & 86

QUAI GRENELLE

Bir-Hakeim

RUE DE LA FEDERATION

AVE. DE SUFFREN

BLVD. DE GRENELLE

R. SAINT-SAENS

RUE DESAIX

RUE E. FAURE

RUE DE PRESLES

R. DUPLEIX

FAT TIRE TOURS

N

400 Meters

RUE DANIEL STERN

Square Dupleix

400 Yards

Dupleix

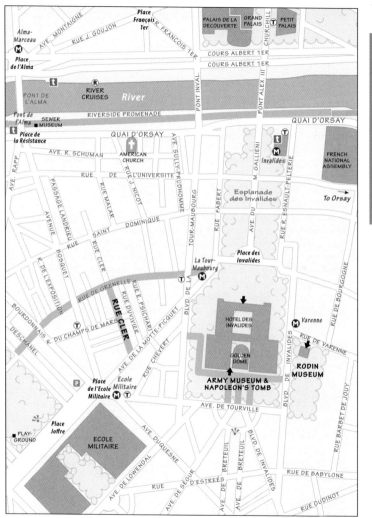

the river, Mo: Alma-Marceau, RER/Train-C: Pont de l'Alma, +33 1 53 68 27 81.

▲▲Rue Cler

Paris is always changing, but a stroll down this market street introduces you to a thriving, traditional Parisian neighborhood and offers insights into the local culture.

    📖 See the Rue Cler Walk chapter.

▲▲Army Museum and Napoleon's Tomb (Musée de l'Armée)

The complex of Les Invalides—a former veterans' hospital built by Louis XIV—has Napoleon's tomb and Europe's greatest military museum. Here you can watch the art of war unfold from stone axes to Axis powers.

At the center of the complex, Napoleon Bonaparte lies majestically dead inside several coffins under a grand dome—a goose bump-inducing pilgrimage for historians. Your visit continues through an impressive range of museums filled with medieval armor, cannons and muskets, Louis XIV-era uniforms and weapons, and Napoleon's horse—stuffed and mounted.

The best section is dedicated to the two World Wars. Walk chronologically through displays on the trench warfare of World War I, the victory parades, France's horrendous losses, and the humiliating Treaty of Versailles that led to World War II. The WWII rooms use black-and-white photos, maps, videos, and a few artifacts to trace Hitler's rise, the Blitzkrieg that overran France, America's entry into the war, D-Day, the concentration camps, the atomic bomb, the war in the Pacific, and the eventual Allied victory. There's special insight into France's role (the French Resistance), and how it was Charles de Gaulle who actually won the war.

▶ *€14, covered by Museum Pass; daily 10:00-18:00, Napoleon's Tomb open until 21:00 on Tue; multimedia guide-€5; 129 Rue de Grenelle, Mo: La Tour Maubourg, Varenne, or Invalides; +33 1 44 42 38 77, www. musee-armee.fr.*

▲▲Rodin Museum (Musée Rodin)

This user-friendly museum with gardens is filled with passionate works by Auguste Rodin (1840-1917), the greatest sculptor since

Rodin Museum—*The Kiss, The Thinker,* and more The Army Museum's WWII wing

Michelangelo. You'll see *The Kiss, The Thinker, The Gates of Hell,* and many more, well displayed in the mansion where the sculptor lived and worked.

Rodin sculpted human figures on an epic scale, revealing through their bodies his deepest thoughts and feelings. Like many of Michelangelo's unfinished works, Rodin's statues rise from the raw stone around them, driven by the life force. With missing limbs and scarred skin, these are prefab classics, making ugliness noble. Rodin's people are always moving restlessly. Even the famous *Thinker* is moving; while he's plopped down solidly, his mind is a million miles away.

Exhibits trace Rodin's artistic development, explain how his bronze statues were cast, and show some of the studies he created to work up to his masterpiece, the unfinished *Gates of Hell.* Learn about Rodin's tumultuous relationship with his apprentice and lover, Camille Claudel. Mull over what makes his sculptures some of the most evocative since the Renaissance. And stroll the beautiful gardens, packed with many of his greatest works (including *The Thinker*) and ideal for artistic reflection.

▶ *€13, free first Sun of the month Oct-March, €24 combo-ticket with Orsay Museum, covered by Museum Pass; Tue-Sun 10:00-18:30, closed Mon, Oct-March garden closes at dusk; audioguide-€6, 77 Rue de Varenne, Mo: Varenne, +33 1 44 18 61 10, www.musee-rodin.fr.*

▲▲Marmottan Museum (Musée Marmottan Monet)

In this private, intimate, and untouristy museum, you'll find the best collection anywhere of works by Impressionist headliner Claude Monet. Follow Monet's life through more than a hundred works, from simple sketches to the *Impression: Sunrise* painting that gave his

Best Views over the City of Light

Eiffel Tower: The ultimate. Period.

Paris Ferris Wheel: Offers a 200-foot-high view of Paris.

Arc de Triomphe: Best at night, when the Champs-Elysées glitters.

Steps of Sacré-Cœur: Walk uphill, or take the funicular to join the party on Paris' only hilltop.

Galeries Lafayette or **Printemps:** Both department stores have a stunning overlook of the old Opéra district.

Montparnasse Tower: This solitary skyscraper's views are best by day.

Pompidou Center: Great views plus exciting modern art.

Place du Trocadéro: It's at street level but is the best place to see the Eiffel Tower.

Windo Skybar at Hôtel Hyatt Regency Paris Etoile: This otherwise unappealing hotel's 34th-floor bar has a stunning Parisian panorama.

artistic movement its start—and a name. The museum also displays some of the enjoyable large-scale canvases featuring the water lilies from his garden at Giverny.

The Marmottan also features a world-class collection of works by Berthe Morisot and other Impressionists, and an eclectic collection of non-Monet objects, such as furniture and illuminated manuscript drawings.

▶ *€12, not covered by Museum Pass, ask about combo-ticket with Monet's garden and house at Giverny; Tue-Sun 10:00-18:00, Thu until 21:00, closed Mon; audioguide-€4, 2 Rue Louis-Boilly, Mo: La Muette, +33 1 44 96 50 33, www.marmottan.fr.*

LEFT BANK

▲Latin Quarter (Quartier Latin)

This Left Bank neighborhood, immediately across the river from Notre-Dame, was the center of Roman Paris. But the Latin Quarter's touristy fame relates to its intriguing, artsy, bohemian character. This

was perhaps Europe's leading university district in the Middle Ages, when Latin was the language of higher education. The neighborhood's main boulevards (St. Michel and St. Germain) are lined with cafés—once the haunts of great poets and philosophers, now the hangouts of tired tourists. Though still youthful and artsy, much of this area is touristy and filled with cheap North African eateries.

▲▲Cluny Museum (Musée National du Moyen Age)

This treasure trove of Middle Ages (Moyen Age) art fills old Roman baths, offering close-up looks at stained glass, Notre-Dame carvings, fine goldsmithing and jewelry, and rooms of tapestries. The star here is the exquisite series of six *Lady and the Unicorn* tapestries: A delicate, as-medieval-as-can-be noble lady introduces a delighted unicorn to the senses of taste, hearing, sight, smell, and touch. The sixth is

Head to the Cluny Museum for medieval art.

Luxembourg Garden—an urban oasis

the most talked-about tapestry: *A Mon Seul Désir (To My Sole Desire)*. What is the lady's only desire? Is it that jewel box, or is it something—or someone—inside that tent? Human sensuality is awakening, an old dark age is ending, and the Renaissance is emerging.

▶ *€12, free on first Sun of the month, covered by Museum Pass; Tue-Sun 9:30-18:15, closed Mon, last entry 45 minutes before closing; 6 Place Paul Painlevé, Mo: Cluny La Sorbonne, St-Michel, or Odéon; +33 1 53 73 78 10, www.musee-moyenage.fr.*

▲St. Sulpice Church

For pipe-organ enthusiasts, a visit here is one of Europe's great musical treats. The Grand Orgue at St. Sulpice Church has a rich history, with a succession of 12 world-class organists that goes back 300 years. Patterned after St. Paul's Cathedral in London, the church has a Neoclassical arcaded facade and two round towers. Inside, in the first chapel on the right, are three murals of fighting angels by Delacroix: *Jacob Wrestling the Angel, Heliodorus Chased from the Temple,* and *The Archangel Michael* (on the ceiling). The fourth chapel on the right has a statue of Joan of Arc and wall plaques listing hundreds from St. Sulpice's congregation who died during World War I.

You can hear the organ played before and after Sunday Mass (10:45-11:00, 12:00-12:30, and 18:35; dress appropriately), followed by a high-powered 25-minute recital, usually performed by talented organist Daniel Roth.

▶ *Free, daily 7:30-19:30, Mo: St-Sulpice or Mabillon. See www.aross.fr/ en for special concerts.*

▲Luxembourg Garden (Jardin du Luxembourg)

This lovely 60-acre garden is an Impressionist painting brought to life. Slip into a green chair pondside, enjoy the radiant flower beds, go jogging, play tennis or basketball, sail a toy sailboat, or take in a chess game or puppet show. The garden, dotted with fountains and statues, is the property of the French Senate, which meets here in Luxembourg Palace. There's no better place to watch Parisians at play.

▶ *Open daily dawn until dusk, Mo: Odéon, RER/Train-B: Luxembourg.*

▲Panthéon

This state-capitol-style Neoclassical monument celebrates France's illustrious history and people, balances a Foucault pendulum, and is the final resting place of many French VIPs.

Inside the vast, evenly lit space—360 feet long, 280 feet wide, and 270 feet high—monuments trace the celebrated struggles of the French people: a beheaded St. Denis (painting on left wall of nave), St. Geneviève saving the fledgling city from Attila the Hun, and scenes of Joan of Arc (left transept). A Foucault pendulum swings gracefully at the end of a cable suspended from the towering dome. It was here in 1851 that the scientist Léon Foucault first demonstrated the rotation of the earth. A panoply of greats is in the crypt: Rousseau, Voltaire, Victor Hugo, Alexandre Dumas, Louis Braille, and Marie Curie. It's 206 steps to the base of the dome for views of the interior and the city.

▶ *€11.50, covered by Museum Pass, €3.50 for dome climb (not covered by Museum Pass); daily 10:00-18:30, Oct-March until 18:00, last entry 45 minutes before closing; audioguide-€3, Mo: Cardinal Lemoine, +33 1 44 32 18 00, http://pantheon.monuments-nationaux.fr.*

Montparnasse Tower

This sadly out-of-place 59-story superscraper has one virtue: If you can't make it up the Eiffel Tower, the sensational views from this tower are cheaper, far easier to access, and make for a fair consolation prize. Come early in the day for clearest skies and shortest lines and be treated to views from a comfortable interior and from up on the rooftop. Sunset is great but views are disappointing after dark.

▶ *€20, RS%—30 percent discount (2 people per book), not covered by Museum Pass; daily 10:00-23:30, Oct-March 11:00-22:30; entrance on Rue de l'Arrivée, Mo: Montparnasse-Bienvenüe—from the Métro, stay* *inside the station and follow signs to exit #1, +33 1 45 38 52 56, www. tourmontparnasse56.com.*

▲Catacombs

Spiral down 60 feet below the street and walk a one-mile route through tunnels containing the anonymous bones of six million permanent Parisians.

In 1785, health-conscious Parisians looking to relieve congestion and improve the city's sanitary conditions emptied the church cemeteries and moved the bones here, to former limestone quarries. The bones are stacked in piles five feet high and as much as 80 feet deep.

Descend 130 steps and ponder the sign announcing, "Halt, this is the empire of the dead." Shuffle along passageways of artfully arranged, skull-studded tibiae and see more cheery signs: "Happy is he who is forever faced with the hour of his death and prepares himself for the end every day." Then climb many steps to emerge far from where you entered, with white-limestone-covered toes, telling everyone you've been underground gawking at bones. Note to wannabe Hamlets: An attendant checks your bag at the exit for stolen souvenirs.

▶ *€29, book online in advance, includes audioguide, not covered by Museum Pass; Tue-Sun 10:00-20:30, closed Mon; €15 same-day tickets sometimes available online and on-site; enter at 1 Place Denfert-Rochereau, Mo: Denfert-Rochereau, +33 1 43 22 47 63, www.catacombes. paris.fr.*

CHAMPS-ELYSEES AND NEARBY

▲▲▲Champs-Elysées

This famous boulevard is Paris' backbone, with its greatest concentration of traffic (although it's delightfully traffic-free on the first Sun of the month). And though the Champs-Elysées has become as international as it is Parisian, a walk down the two-mile boulevard is still a must.

In 1667, Louis XIV opened the first section of the street, and it soon became the place to cruise in your carriage. (It still is today.) By the 1920s, this boulevard was pure elegance—fancy residences, rich hotels, and cafés. Today it's home to big business, celebrity cafés, glitzy nightclubs, high-fashion shopping, and international people-watching.

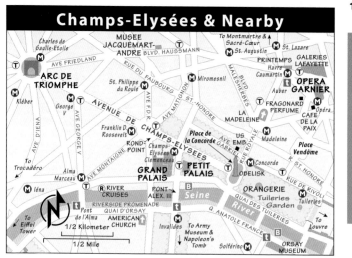

Map labels: Charles de Gaulle-Etoile, MUSÉE JACQUEMART-ANDRE, AVE FRIEDLAND, RUE DU FAUBOURG, BLVD. HAUSSMANN, To Montmartre & Sacré-Cœur, St. Augustin, St. Lazare, PRINTEMPS, GALERIES LAFAYETTE, Caumartin, ARC DE TRIOMPHE, St. Philippe du Roule, Miromesnil, Auber, OPÉRA GARNIER, Opéra, Kléber, George V, AVENUE DE CHAMPS-ELYSÉES, AVE D.F.R., ST.-HONORE, FRAGONARD PERFUME, LA MADELEINE, CAFÉ DE LA PAIX, AVE DIENA, AVE GEORGE V, Franklin D. Roosevelt, ROND-POINT, Champs-Elysées Clemenceau, Place de la Concorde, AVE GABRIEL, US EMB., Madeleine, RUE ROYALE, Place Vendôme, To Trocadéro, Alma Marceau, AVE MONTAIGNE, GRAND PALAIS, PETIT PALAIS, Concorde, OBELISK, RUE ST.-HONORE, RUE DE RIVOLI, Iéna, RIVER CRUISES, PONT ALEX. III, Seine, ORANGERIE, Tuileries Garden, Tuileries, To Louvre, RIVERSIDE PROMENADE, QUAI D'ORSAY, River, Q. ANATOLE FRANCE, To Eiffel Tower, Pont de l'Alma, AMERICAN CHURCH, 1/2 Kilometer, Invalides, To Army Museum & Napoleon's Tomb, Solférino, ORSAY MUSEUM, 1/2 Mile

SIGHTS

Start at the Arc de Triomphe and walk down the north side of the street. The Lido (#116) is Paris' largest burlesque-type cabaret (and a multiplex cinema). Across the boulevard is the flagship store of leather-bag maker Louis Vuitton (#101). Fouquet's café (#99) is a popular spot for French celebrities, especially movie stars—note the names in the sidewalk in front. Enter if you dare for a pricey espresso. Ladurée café (#75) is also classy but has a welcoming and affordable takeout bakery.

Continuing on, you pass international-brand stores, such as Sephora, Disney, and Renault. You can end your walk at the round Rond Point intersection (Mo: Franklin D. Roosevelt) or continue to obelisk-studded Place de la Concorde.

▲▲Arc de Triomphe

Napoleon had the magnificent Arc de Triomphe commissioned to commemorate his victory at the 1805 battle of Austerlitz. The foot of the arch is a stage on which the last two centuries of Parisian history have played out—from the funeral of Napoleon to the goose-stepping arrival of the Nazis to the triumphant return of Charles de Gaulle after the Allied liberation. Examine the carvings on the pillars, featuring a

Champs-Elysées with Arc de Triomphe

Opéra Garnier's grand staircase

mighty Napoleon and excitable Lady Liberty. Pay your respects at the Tomb of the Unknown Soldier where, every day at 18:30, the flame is rekindled and new flowers set in place.

Now climb the 284 steps to the observation deck up top, with sweeping skyline panoramas and a mesmerizing view down onto the traffic that swirls around the arch. You're at the center of a grand axis of city planning, stretching from the Louvre, up the Champs-Elysées to the Arc de Triomphe, then continuing west to the huge, rectangular, modern Grande Arche de la Défense. Looking down you see 12 converging boulevards forming a star (*étoile*). What a traffic mess! Or is it? Cars entering the circle have the right of way; those in the circle must yield.

▶ *€13 to climb to the rooftop, timed-entry tickets available online, free on first Sun of the month Nov-March, covered by Museum Pass—pass holders do not need to reserve a time slot; daily 10:00-23:00, Oct-March until 22:30, last entry 45 minutes before closing; Place Charles de Gaulle, use underpass to reach arch, Mo: Charles de Gaulle-Etoile, +33 1 55 37 73 77, www.paris-arc-de-triomphe.fr.*

▲Petit Palais (and Musée des Beaux-Arts)

This free museum displays a broad collection of paintings and sculpture from the 1600s to the 1900s on its ground floor, and an easy-to-appreciate collection of art from Greek antiquities to Art Nouveau in its basement. There are a few diamonds in the rough, including Courbet's soft-porn *The Sleepers* (*Le Sommeil*, 1866), which captures two women nestled in post-climactic bliss; Monet's *Sunset on the Seine at Lavacourt* (*Soleil couchant sur la Seine a Lavacourt*, 1880), painted the winter after his wife died; and works by the American painter Mary Cassatt and other Impressionists.

▶ *Free, Tue-Sun 10:00-18:00, Fri until 21:00 for special exhibits (fee), closed Mon; across from Grand Palais on Avenue Winston Churchill, Mo: Champs-Elysées Clemenceau; +33 1 53 43 40 00, www.petitpalais. paris.fr.*

SIGHTS

▲Paris Ferris Wheel (Roue de Paris)

In summer, the Paris Ferris Wheel offers a sensational 200-foot-high view of the city from the northern side of the Tuileries Garden. The towering wheel is the centerpiece of a funfair complete with kid-pleasing rides and games.

▶ *€12 ticket covers two slow revolutions, two passengers per gondola, open long hours daily late June-late Aug.*

OPERA NEIGHBORHOOD

▲▲Opéra Garnier

A gleaming grand theater of the belle époque, the Palais Garnier was built for Napoleon III and finished in 1875. For the best exterior view, stand in front of the Opéra Métro stop. The building is huge. Its massive foundations straddle an underground lake (inspiring the mysterious world of *The Phantom of the Opera*). It's the masterpiece of architect Charles Garnier, who oversaw every element, from the laying of the foundations to what color the wallpaper should be.

To see the interior, you can take a guided tour (your best look), tour the public areas on your own (using the audioguide), or attend a performance. Note that the auditorium is sometimes off-limits due to performances and rehearsals. Highlights of the interior include the Grand Staircase, the various chandeliered reception halls, the 2,000-seat auditorium, and a few exhibits on the building and opera. The climax of the visit is a view from the upper seats into the red-velvet performance hall. There you can see Marc Chagall's colorful ceiling (1964) and a seven-ton chandelier.

Near the Opéra are the Fragonard Perfume Museum (free, 3 Square Louis Jouvet), the venerable Galeries Lafayette department store, and the glitterati-flecked Café de la Paix (5 Place de l'Opéra).

▶ *€14, €4 off with Orsay Museum ticket (within 8 days of Orsay visit),* *not covered by Museum Pass; generally daily 10:00-16:15, mid-July-Aug until 17:15; guided tour in English usually daily at 14:00, reserve online, arrive 30 minutes early for security screening; 8 Rue Scribe, Mo: Opéra, RER/Train-A: Auber, www.operadeparis.fr/en/visits/palais-garnier.*

For performances, ask for a schedule at the information booth, the Paris Opera website (www.operadeparis.fr), or the ticket office (open Mon-Sat 11:30–18:30 and an hour before the show, closed Sun).

▲▲Jacquemart-André Museum
(Musée Jacquemart-André)

This enjoyable (if somewhat faded) museum-mansion, with an elegant café, showcases the lavish home of a wealthy, art-loving, 19th-century Parisian couple. Edouard André and his wife Nélie Jacquemart spent their lives and fortunes designing, building, and then decorating this sumptuous mansion. The place is strewn with paintings by Rembrandt, Botticelli, Uccello, Mantegna, Bellini, Boucher, and Fragonard. Though there are no must-see masterpieces, the art gathered here would still be enough to make any gallery famous.

The sumptuous museum tearoom serves delicious cakes and tea. From here walk north on Rue de Courcelles to see Paris' most beautiful park, Parc Monceau.

▸ *€12, €3-5 more for special exhibits, includes audioguide, not covered by Museum Pass; daily 10:00-18:00, Mon until 20:30 during special exhibits; purchase tickets online in advance (€2 fee), 158 Boulevard Haussmann, Mo: St-Philippe-du-Roule; +33 1 45 62 11 59, www.musee-jacquemart-andre.com.*

MARAIS NEIGHBORHOOD AND MORE

▲Strolling the Marais

With more pre-Revolutionary lanes and mansions than anywhere else in town, the Marais is more atmospheric than touristy. In the 1600s, this former swamp (*marais*) became home to aristocrats' private mansions (*hôtels*), located close to the king's townhouse on stylish Place des Vosges. With the Revolution, the Marais turned working-class, filled with artisans and immigrants, and became home to

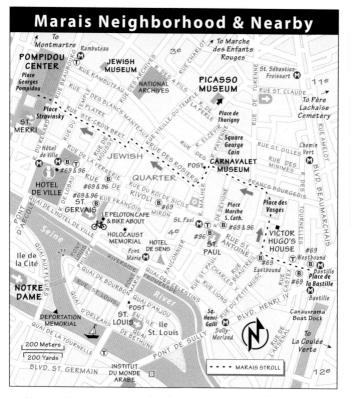

SIGHTS

Paris' Jewish community. Today the area is trendy and home to young professionals.

For a good east-to-west introductory walk (see the map), start at Place de la Bastille (nightlife) and head west on busy Rue Saint-Antoine to Place des Vosges (art galleries, restaurants). Continue west on Rue des Francs-Bourgeois (fashion boutiques), turning onto Rue des Rosiers (Jewish neighborhood) and Rue Ste. Croix de la Bretonnerie (gay Paree's LGBTQ community) to the Pompidou Center. On Sunday afternoons, the area pulses with shoppers and café crowds.

▲Place des Vosges

Henry IV built this centerpiece of the Marais in 1605 and called it "Place Royale." As he'd hoped, it turned the Marais into Paris' most exclusive neighborhood. In the center, a statue of Louis XIII, on horseback, gestures, "Look at this wonderful square my dad built." He's surrounded by locals enjoying their community park, children frolicking in the sandbox, lovers warming benches, and pigeons guarding their fountains while trees shade this escape from the glare of the big city. Around the square, arcades shade cafés and art galleries.

Study the architecture: nine pavilions (houses) per side. The two highest—at the front and back—were for the king and queen (but were never used). Warm red brickwork—some real, some fake—is topped with sloped slate roofs, chimneys, and another quaint relic of a bygone era: TV antennas.

At 6 Place des Vosges is Victor Hugo's House, a free museum dedicated to France's literary giant (described later). This was where he wrote much of his most important work, including *Les Misérables*.

▲▲Carnavalet Museum (Musée Carnavalet)

Housed in three floors of an elegant mansion, this museum delves into the history of Paris—all wonderfully explained with English descriptions, making it quite user-friendly (once you figure out the confusing floorplan). You get a good overview of everything—from Louis XIV-period rooms, to Napoleon, to the belle époque. But I'd focus on the museum's highlight: the French Revolution and the 19th century.

On the top floor, find the section called "The French Revolution to the 21st Century." Each room starts with a concise historic recap, with displays that are both fascinating and well-described in English. You'll see the roots of revolution, divine monarchs and angry masses, the Bastille prison, royals who lost their heads, revolutionary heroes, the Reign of Terror, and Napoleon.

Popping out the other end, a curvy wooden staircase leads down to another fascinating era: "Paris 1852 to Today." You'll wind through a series of rooms that illustrate the foundations of the Paris we know and love today. The exhibit starts with Baron Haussmann and his late-19th-century redesign of the city, then traces the *fin de siècle* and beyond: can-can dancers, the Eiffel Tower, hot-air balloons, the belle époque, Art Nouveau, and the Impressionists.

▸ *Free, Tue-Sun 10:00-18:00, closed Mon, 16 Rue des Francs Bourgeois, Mo: St-Paul, www.carnavalet.paris.fr.*

▲Picasso Museum (Musée Picasso)

Whatever you think about Picasso the man, as an artist he was unmatched in the 20th century for his daring and productivity. This museum rotates its huge collection of Picasso works to host an ever-changing calendar of Picasso-themed exhibits.

▸ *€14, covered by Museum Pass, free on first Sun of month; Tue-Fri 10:30-18:00, Sat-Sun from 9:30, closed Mon, last entry 45 minutes before closing; 5 Rue de Thorigny, Mo: St-Sébastien-Froissart, St-Paul, or Chemin Vert, +33 1 42 71 25 21, www.museepicassoparis.fr.*

▲Jewish Art and History Museum (Musée d'Art et Histoire du Judaïsme)

This is a fine museum of historical artifacts and rare ritual objects spanning the Jewish people's long cultural heritage. It emphasizes the cultural unity maintained by this continually dispersed population. You'll learn about Jewish traditions and see exquisite costumes and objects central to daily life and religious practices. Those with a background in Judaism or who take the time with the thoughtful audioguide and posted information will be rewarded.

▸ *€10, includes audioguide, covered by Museum Pass, free on first Sat of month Oct-June; Tue-Fri 11:00-18:00, Sat-Sun from 10:00, open later during special exhibits—Wed until 21:00 and Sat-Sun until 19:00, closed Mon year-round, last entry 45 minutes before closing; 71 Rue du Temple, Mo: Rambuteau or Hôtel de Ville; +33 1 53 01 86 60, www.mahj.org.*

▲▲Pompidou Center (Centre Pompidou)

Some people hate modern art. But the Pompidou Center contains what is possibly Europe's best collection of 20th-century art. In addition, the occasional temporary exhibitions, the great rooftop view, and the perpetual street fair of performers and crêpe stands outside all make this museum worthwhile.

The colorful building is exoskeletal (like a crab or Notre-Dame), with its functional parts—the pipes, heating ducts, and escalator—on

Place des Vosges—the heart of the Marais

Pompidou—wild and crazy modern art

the outside, and the meaty art inside. It's the epitome of modern architecture, where "form follows function."

The permanent collection (on the fourth and fifth floors) features all the big names of the early 20th century—Matisse, Picasso, Chagall, Dalí—and continues with contemporary art. This art was ahead of its time and is still waiting for the world to catch up. After so many Madonnas-and-children, a piano smashed to bits and glued to the wall is refreshing. Once you've seen the permanent collection, explore the temporary exhibits to connect with what is "now" from around the globe.

Note that the museum is scheduled to close in late 2024 for a multiyear facelift.

▶ €14, free on first Sun of the month, €5 for escalator to sixth-floor view (but no museum entry); Museum Pass covers permanent collection and sixth-floor panoramic views (plus occasional special exhibits); permanent collection open Wed-Mon 11:00-21:00, closed Tue, ticket counters close at 20:00; rest of the building open until 22:00 (Thu until 23:00); arrive after 17:00 to avoid crowds; Mo: Rambuteau or Hôtel de Ville, +33 1 44 78 12 33, www.centrepompidou.fr.

▲▲Père Lachaise Cemetery (Cimetière du Père Lachaise)

Littered with the tombstones of many of the city's most illustrious dead, this is your best one-stop look at Paris' fascinating, romantic past residents. More like a small city, the cemetery is big and confusing. It's smart to buy a grave-locator map from florists across from the Porte Gambetta entrance. Use it to find the graves of Frédéric Chopin (the Polish pianist whose tomb always sports fresh flowers), Molière (playwright to Louis XIV), Edith Piaf (warbling singer who regretted

Chopin's grave at Père Lachaise Cemetery

Montmartre, capped with Sacré-Cœur

nothing), Oscar Wilde (controversial figure who died in Paris), Jim Morrison (ditto), Gertrude Stein (American writer), Héloïse and Abélard (illicit medieval lovers), and many more.

▶ *Free, Mon-Fri 8:00-18:00, Sat from 8:30, Sun from 9:00, closes at 17:30 in winter; two blocks from Mo: Gambetta (do not go to Mo: Père Lachaise); +33 1 55 25 82 10, searchable map available at unofficial website: www.pere-lachaise.com.*

Victor Hugo's House (Maison Victor Hugo)

France's literary giant lived in this house on Place des Vosges from 1832 to 1848. Hugo stayed in many places during his life, but he was here the longest. He moved to this apartment after the phenomenal success of *The Hunchback of Notre-Dame,* and it was while living here that he wrote much of *Les Misérables* (when he wasn't entertaining Paris' elite). After climbing up two floors, you'll visit well-decorated rooms re-creating different phases of Hugo's life and passions, from his celebrity years, to his 19-year exile during the repressive reign of Napoleon III (Hugo said, "When freedom returns, I will return."), to his final years as a national treasure. Rooms are littered with personal possessions and paintings of Hugo and his family and of some of his most famous character creations. Posted explanations in English provide sufficient context to grasp the importance of Hugo to France.

▶ *Free, fee for optional special exhibits, Tue-Sun 10:00-18:00, closed Mon, courtyard café, good WCs, 6 Place des Vosges; Mo: Bastille, St-Paul, or Chemin Vert; +33 1 42 72 10 16, http://maisonsvictorhugo. paris.fr.*

Montmartre, Paris' highest hill, is topped by Sacré-Cœur Basilica and is best known as the home of cabaret nightlife and bohemian artists. Struggling painters, poets, dreamers, and drunkards came here for cheap rent, untaxed booze, rustic landscapes, and views of the underwear of high-kicking cancan girls at the Moulin Rouge. These days, the hill is equal parts charm and kitsch—still vaguely village-like but mobbed with tourists and pickpockets—especially on sunny weekends. Come for a bit of history, a getaway from Paris' noisy boulevards, and the view (to beat the crowds, it's best on a weekday or early on weekend mornings).

Start your visit at the **Sacré-Cœur** (Sacred Heart) Basilica. The striking exterior, with its onion domes and bleached-bone pallor, looks ancient, but it was finished only a century ago. Inside, you'll see impressive mosaics (including one of Jesus with his sacred heart burning with love and compassion for humanity), a statue of St. Thérèse, a scale model of the church, and three stained-glass windows dedicated to Joan of Arc. For an unobstructed panoramic view of Paris, climb 260 feet (300 steps) up the tight and claustrophobic spiral stairs to the top of the dome (church—free, daily 6:30-22:30; dome—€7, not covered by Museum Pass, daily 10:00-18:00, June-Sept until 20:00, Jan-Feb until 17:00; modest dress required; Mo: Anvers; +33 1 53 41 89 00, www.sacre-coeur-montmartre.com).

Montmartre's main square, **Place du Tertre,** one block from the church, was once the haunt of Henri de Toulouse-Lautrec and the original bohemians. Today, it's crawling with tourists and unoriginal bohemians.

The **Montmartre Museum** re-creates the traditional cancan-and-cabaret scene, with paintings, posters, photos, music, videos, and memorabilia; plus it offers the chance to see the studio of Maurice Utrillo (€14, includes good audioguide, not covered by Museum Pass; Wed-Mon 10:00-18:00, closed Tue, last entry 45 minutes before closing; 12 Rue Cortot, +33 1 49 25 89 39, www.museedemontmartre.fr).

A few blocks away are the historic **Au Lapin Agile** cabaret (still in business) and the **Moulin de la Galette,** a dance hall featured in a famous Renoir painting at the Orsay. Wandering the neighborhood, you can see the (boring) exteriors of former homes of Picasso, Toulouse-Lautrec, Van Gogh, and composer Erik Satie.

Chartres' cathedral—pure Gothic glory

At the base of the hill (near Mo: Blanche), the **Moulin Rouge** ("Red Windmill") nightclub still offers glitzy, pricey shows to busloads of tourists. The neighborhood around it, called Pigalle, is Paris' red light district, but it's more racy than dangerous.

DAY TRIPS FROM PARIS

▲▲▲Versailles
Twelve miles southwest of Paris, the jaw-dropping residence of French kings features a lavish palace and expansive, fountain-dotted gardens.
  📖 See the Versailles Tour chapter.

▲▲Chartres: The Town and the Cathedral
One of Europe's greatest Gothic cathedrals soars above the pleasant town of Chartres, an hour southwest of Paris.
▶ *Catch the train from Paris' Gare Montparnasse (14/day, about €16 one-way). The church is free and open daily 8:30-19:30.*

A Page of History

The Beginnings (AD 1-1500): Julius Caesar conquered the Parisii, turning Paris from a tribal fishing village into a European city. The mix of Latin (southern) and Celtic (northern) cultures, with Paris in the middle, defined the French character. Roman Paris fell to the Franks (hence "France") and Norsemen ("Normans"). Charlemagne (768-814) briefly united the Franks, giving a glimpse of modern France. In 1066, William the Conqueror awkwardly united England and France, bringing centuries of border wars. Eventually, Joan of Arc (1412-1431) rallied the French to drive the English out. Modern France was born.

France Dominates (1500-1789): Renaissance kings François I and Henry IV established France as a European power, and Louis XIV made it a superpower. Under Louis XV and XVI, every educated European spoke French and followed French aristocratic customs. Meanwhile, enlightened French philosophers sowed the seeds of democracy.

Revolution (1789-1800): On July 14, 1789, Parisian revolutionaries stormed the Bastille, and eventually beheaded the king and queen. Thousands were guillotined if suspected of hindering democracy. From the chaos rose a charismatic commoner: Napoleon Bonaparte.

Elected Emperors and Constitutional Kings (1800s): Napoleon conquered Europe, crowned himself emperor, and invaded Russia, before being defeated at Waterloo. The monarchy was restored, but rulers had to toe the democratic line. Eventually, Napoleon's nephew (Napoleon III) presided over a wealthy-but-declining era of big monuments and Impressionist art, known as the belle époque—the "beautiful age."

War and Depression (1900-1950): Two world wars with Germany wasted the country. France lost millions of men in World War I and was easily overrun by Hitler in World War II. Paris, now dirt cheap, attracted foreign writers (Hemingway) and artists (Picasso).

Postwar France (1950-Present): France recovered slowly under wartime hero Charles de Gaulle. As its colonial empire dissolved after bitter wars in Algeria and Vietnam, immigrants flooded Paris. The turbulent '60s, progressive '70s, socialist-turned-conservative '80s, and the middle-of-the-road '90s brought us to the 21st century. Paris has regained its place as one of the world's great cities.

Claude Monet's iconic garden and pond at Giverny

▲Giverny

Claude Monet's garden still looks like it did when he painted it. Wander among the flowers, the rose trellis, the Japanese Bridge, and the pond filled with lily pads.

▶ *Minivan or big bus tours are the easiest way to get there (€80-120). On your own, drive or take the Rouen-bound train from Gare St. Lazare to Vernon (about hourly, about €30 round-trip, 1 hour). From Vernon, take the public bus (generally runs every 2 hours, €10 round-trip, www.giverny.org/transpor), a taxi (€20 one-way), or rent a bike at the café opposite the train station (closed Mon).*

Monet's Garden and House are open daily 9:30-18:00, closed Nov-late March (€11, not covered by Museum Pass, ask about combo-tickets with Paris' Orangerie or Marmottan Museums; +33 2 32 51 90 31, http://fondation-monet.com).

Activities

You'll never run out of things to do in Paris. This chapter offers suggestions for tours, shopping, and entertainment. For a relaxing cultural overview, consider a cruise on the Seine or a leisurely bus tour. Bike and walking tours range from the traditional (art and architecture) to the obscure (history of the baguette).

As they race from museum to monument, visitors often miss Paris' market streets and village-like charm. Give yourself a vacation from sightseeing with a stroll through a Parisian neighborhood, feeling the rhythm of daily life. Save energy to experience the City of Light after dark. Whether it's a concert at Sainte-Chapelle, a boat ride on the Seine, a walk in Montmartre, a hike up the Arc de Triomphe, or a late-night café, you'll see Paris at its best.

TOURS

🎧 To sightsee on your own, download my **free audio tours** that illuminate some of Paris' top sights and neighborhoods (see the sidebar on page 12).

Hop-On, Hop-Off Bus Tours

Double-decker bus services connect Paris' main sights, giving you an easy once-over of the city with a basic recorded commentary. You can hop off at any stop, tour a sight, then hop on a later bus. It's dang scenic—if you get a top-deck seat and the weather's decent. But because of traffic and stops, these buses are slooooow. (Busy sightseers will do better using the Métro.) Buy tickets from the driver or online (€36-39 for one day). **TootBus** has a well-designed, 10-stop route covering central Paris (www.tootbus.com). Also consider **Big Bus Paris** (www.bigbustours.com).

Seine Cruises

Several companies run one-hour boat cruises on the Seine. A typical cruise loops back and forth between the Eiffel Tower and Pont d'Austerlitz and costs about €15-17. For a fun experience, cruise at twilight or after dark. **Bateaux-Mouches** cruises depart from Pont de l'Alma and have the biggest open-top, double-decker boats (often crowded, www.bateaux-mouches.fr). **Bateaux Parisiens** (www.bateauxparisiens.com) and **Vedettes de Paris** (www.vedettesdeparis.fr) start and end at the Eiffel Tower, while **Vedettes du Pont Neuf** departs from Pont Neuf (www.vedettesdupontneuf.com).

Walking Tours

Paris Walks offers thoughtful and entertaining two-hour walks led by British and American guides (€15-25, generally 2/day, www.pariswalks.com). **Context Travel**'s private and small group walking tours are for travelers serious about learning (from €120/person, generally 3 hours, www.contexttravel.com).

   Fat Tire Tours offers high-on-fun and casual walking tours. Their two-hour Classic Paris Walking Tour covers most major sights (Mon, Wed, and Fri at 10:00 or 15:00). Their "Skip the Line" tours get you into major sights (such as Versailles) but are most worthwhile for the Eiffel Tower and Catacombs (€25 walking tours, €54-99 "Skip the

Paris offers *beaucoup* ways for you to connect with locals—making your trip more personal...and more memorable. **Meeting the French** links travelers with Parisians who offer specialty tours, trip-organizing help, and more (www.meetingthefrench.com).

Paris Greeter's volunteers show you "their Paris" (www.greeters.paris). The interdenominational **American Church and Franco-American Center,** in the Rue Cler neighborhood, offers many services for travelers wanting to connect with Parisian culture (www.acparis.org). **Lost in Frenchlation** hosts weekly screenings of French films (with English subtitles, www.lostinfrenchlation.com). **Paris by Mouth** offers small-group food tours led by local food writers (www.parisbymouth.com), and **La Cuisine Paris** has a great variety of cooking classes (in English, www.lacuisineparis.com). **Ô Château** has wine-tasting classes in Madame de Pompadour's 18th-century home (www.o-chateau.com).

Line" tours; RS%—€2 discount per person, 2-discount maximum; 24 Rue Edgar Faure, Mo: Dupleix, www.fattiretours.com/paris).

Local Guides

For many, Paris merits hiring a Parisian as a personal tour guide (€240-300 half-day). Try **Thierry Gauduchon** (mobile +33 6 19 07 30 77, tgauduchon@gmail.com), **Elisabeth Van Hest** (mobile +33 6 77 80 19 89, elisa.guide@gmail.com), **Sylvie Moreau** (mobile +33 6 87 02 80 67, sylvie.ja.moreau@gmail.com), or **Arnaud Servignat** (mobile +33 6 68 80 29 05, www.french-guide.com, arnotour@icloud.com).

Bike Tours

Bike About Tours offers easygoing 3.5-hour bike tours. The Hidden Paris tour includes a backstreet spin through the Marais, Latin Quarter, and Ile St. Louis. Their Monuments tour takes you past the Louvre, Eiffel Tower, and other classics (€45, RS%—10 percent discount, shop/café near Hôtel de Ville at 17 Rue du Pont Louis Philippe, Mo: St-Paul, mobile +33 6 18 80 84 92, www.bikeabouttours.com).

Fat Tire Tours runs three-hour bike tours of Paris (€39-44; RS%—€4 discount per person, 2-discount maximum; at 10:30,

April-Oct also at 15:00). Livelier night tours go past floodlit monuments and include a cruise (€44, May-Aug daily at 18:30). Both tours meet at Fat Tire's office at 24 Rue Edgar Faure, near the Eiffel Tower (Mo: Dupleix or La Motte-Picquet-Grenelle, +33 1 82 88 80 96, www.fattiretours.com/paris).

SHOPPING

Shopping in chic Paris is altogether tempting—even reluctant shoppers can find good reasons to indulge. Wandering among elegant boutiques provides a break from the heavy halls of the Louvre and, if you approach it right, a little cultural enlightenment. Even if you don't intend to buy anything, budget some time for window shopping, or, as the French call it, *faire du lèche-vitrines* ("window licking").

Shopping Tips and Etiquette: Entering a small store, greet the clerk with *"Bonjour, Madame/Monsieur"* and bid them *"Au revoir"* when leaving. Before making a purchase, watch the locals to see if self-service is allowed. Ask first before you pick up an item: *"Je peux?"* (zhuh puh), meaning, "Can I?" Don't feel obliged to buy. If a shopkeeper offers assistance, just say, *"Je regarde, merci."* If you know what you want, point to your choice and say, *"S'il vous plaît"* (Please; see voo play). Smaller stores are generally closed on Sunday.

Souvenir Shops

The green riverfront stalls near Notre-Dame sell used books, old posters and postcards, magazines, and other tourist paraphernalia in a romantic setting. You'll find souvenir shops on Rue d'Arcole between Notre-Dame and Hôtel de Ville, on Rue de Rivoli across from the Louvre, around the Pompidou Center, on the streets of Montmartre, and in some department stores.

Grand Department Stores

Like cafés, department stores were invented here. Helpful information desks are usually located at the main entrances near the perfume section (with floor plans in English). Stores generally have affordable restaurants (some with view terraces) and a good selection of fairly priced souvenirs. The **Galeries Lafayette** flagship store is a must-see for its stained-glass belle époque dome and grand, open-air rooftop view (40 Boulevard Haussmann, https://haussmann.galerieslafayette.

Galeries Lafayette—chic shopping

Puces St. Ouen flea market

com). A block to the west is **Printemps,** with cheaper prices and an even better view.

Boutique Strolls

Place de la Madeleine Neighborhood (MO: Madeleine): The ritzy streets connecting several high-priced squares—Place de la Madeleine, Place de la Concorde, Place Vendôme, and Place de l'Opéra—form a miracle mile of gourmet food shops, glittering jewelry stores, posh hotels, exclusive clothing boutiques, and people who spend more on clothes in one day than I do in a good year. Start at Eglise de la Madeleine and stroll counterclockwise around the square. In the northeast corner is where world-famous **Fauchon,** founded in 1886, once stood. This bastion of over-the-top edibles catered to the refined tastes of the rich and famous (but recently closed). Continue counterclockwise around Place de la Madeleine. On the western side of the church, step inside tiny **La Maison de la Truffe** (#19) for a whiff of truffles and to ponder how something so ugly, smelly, and deformed can cost so much. Venerable **Mariage Frères** (#17) demonstrates how good tea can smell and how beautifully it can be displayed. And at **Caviar Kaspia** (#17), you can add caviar, eel, and vodka to your truffle collection. Next up, **Le Grand Café Fauchon** serves meals and pastries in its emblematic pink-and-black interior. The boutique has a good selection of wines, chocolates, and fine groceries. To extend this walk, stroll down Rue Royale and turn left on Rue St. Honoré (**Ladurée,** at #16, is famous for its macarons), then left again on Rue de Castiglione. End on the *très* elegant square, Place Vendôme. To trace the route, see the map on page 152.

Sèvres-Babylone to St. Sulpice (Mo: Sèvres-Babylone): For Left

Bank swank, start at the Bon Marché department store, Paris' oldest (follow the route on the map on page 159). Head down Rue de Sèvres, passing **La Maison du Chocolat** at #19 and **Hermès** (#17, famous for its pricey silk scarves). Across the street at 10 Rue de Sèvres sits the marvelously old-school **Au Sauvignon Café,** well situated for watching smartly coiffed shoppers glide by. Detour up Rue du Cherche-Midi to find Paris' most celebrated bread—beautiful round loaves with designer crust—at the low-key **Poilâne** at #8. Spill into Place St. Sulpice, with its big, twin-tower church and **Café de la Mairie**—a great spot to sip a *café crème* and consider your next move.

Flea Markets

Puces St. Ouen (pews sant-oo-an), at Porte de Clignancourt, is the mother of all flea markets. More than 2,000 vendors sell everything from flamingos to faucets, but mostly intriguing antiques and vintage silver and art. No event brings together the melting-pot population of Paris better than this carnival-like market. Some find it claustrophobic; others find French *diamants*-in-the-rough (Sat 9:00-18:00, Sun from 10:00, Mon 11:00-17:00, closed Tue-Fri, www.marcheauxpuces-saintouen.com). From the Porte de Clignancourt Métro station, follow *Sortie, Marché aux Puces* signs and walk straight out of the Métro down Avenue de la Porte de Clignancourt toward the elevated freeway. Veer left on Rue des Rosiers—the "spine" of the market area—and explore the market from there. **Puces de Vanves** is comparatively tiny, with a more traditional flea-market feel (Sat-Sun 7:00-14:00, closed Mon-Fri, Mo: Porte de Vanves).

Traffic-Free Shopping, Café Streets, and Open-Air Food Markets

Traffic-free street markets overflow with flowers, produce, fish vendors, and butchers, illustrating how most Parisians shopped before there were supermarkets and department stores. **Rue Cler** is refined and upscale (Mo: Ecole Militaire). **Rue Montorgueil,** five blocks from the Pompidou Center, is famous as the last vestige of the once-massive Les Halles market (Mo: Etienne Marcel). **Rue Mouffetard,** several blocks behind the Panthéon, starts at picturesque Place Contrescarpe and becomes more Parisian the farther downhill you go (Mo: Censier Daubenton). In the heart of the Left Bank, try **Rue de Seine** and **Rue de Buci** (Mo: Odéon).

The Montparnasse neighborhood's *marché volant*—a bustling pop-up market

Every Paris neighborhood has a ***marché volant*** ("flying market"), where food stalls take over selected boulevards and squares for one to three mornings each week. These thriving neighborhood markets sell everything from rich cheeses, fresh produce, and wines and liquors to bric-a-brac.

VAT and Customs

Getting a VAT Refund: If you purchase more than €175 worth of goods at a single store, you may be eligible to get a refund of the 21 percent Value-Added Tax (VAT). Get more details from your merchant or see www.ricksteves.com/vat.

Customs for American Shoppers: You can take home $800 worth of items per person duty-free, once every 31 days. You can bring in one liter of alcohol duty-free. For details on allowable goods, customs rules, and duty rates, visit http://help.cbp.gov.

NIGHTLIFE

Paris is brilliant after dark. Perhaps the best after-dark activity is to enjoy a leisurely meal, then stroll historic streets, past floodlit squares and fountains.

Jazz and Blues Clubs

With a lively mix of American, French, and international musicians, Paris is an internationally acclaimed jazz capital. You'll pay €12-25 to enter a jazz club. For listings, visit the *Paris Voice* website (http://parisvoice.com). **Caveau de la Huchette** fills an ancient Latin Quarter cellar with nightly live jazz and frenzied dancing (5 Rue de la Huchette, Mo: St-Michel, +33 1 43 26 65 05, www.caveaudelahuchette. fr). **Au Duc des Lombards** is one of the most popular and respected jazz clubs in Paris, with concerts nightly in a plush theater-like setting (42 Rue des Lombards, +33 1 42 33 22 88, www.ducdeslombards.fr). **Le Sunside,** just a block away, has two little stages (60 Rue des Lombards, +33 1 40 26 46 60, www.sunset-sunside.com).

Classical Concerts

From March through November, these churches regularly host concerts (mostly Baroque-style chamber music): St. Sulpice, St. Germain-des-Prés, La Madeleine, St. Eustache, St. Julien-le-Pauvre, and Sainte-Chapelle. **Sainte-Chapelle** is especially worthwhile for the pleasure of hearing Mozart, Bach, or Vivaldi, surrounded by 800 years of stained glass (unheated—bring a sweater, 8 Boulevard du Palais, Mo: Cité, +33 1 42 77 65 65, www.euromusicproductions.fr).

The opulent Opéra Garnier

Tour in a Deux Chevaux— a magical evening

Opera

The **Opéra Bastille** is the massive modern opera house that dominates Place de la Bastille. Come here for state-of-the-art special effects and modern interpretations (Mo: Bastille). The **Opéra Garnier,** Paris' first opera house, hosts opera and ballet performances in a grand belle époque setting (Mo: Opéra). Get tickets for either opera house online at www.operadeparis.fr.

Evening Sightseeing

Some museums (Orsay, Pompidou, Marmottan, and possibly the Louvre) are open late on certain evenings—called *visites nocturnes*—offering more relaxed, less crowded visits. An elaborate sound-and-light show (Les Grandes Eaux Nocturnes) takes place in the gardens at Versailles on some Saturday evenings in summer.

Tours by Night

Consider an evening Seine River cruise or bus tour. Two companies take up to three people on informal, fun, off-beat tours in old Deux Chevaux cars: **4 Roues Sous 1 Parapluie** (+33 6 67 32 26 68, www.4roues-sous-1parapluie.com); **Paris Authentic** (www.parisauthentic.com). Do-it-yourselfers could snag a taxi or Uber and make their own scenic tour—from Notre-Dame to the Eiffel Tower along the Left Bank, then returning along the Right Bank (about €50 for a one-hour loop by taxi, €40 by Uber).

Night Scenes

The Eiffel Tower viewed from Place du Trocadéro is spectacular at night, and the Trocadéro is a festival of hawkers, gawkers, and entertainers. The Champs-Elysées and Arc de Triomphe glitter after dark. Ile St. Louis (Mo: Pont Marie) is quiet and romantic; perfect for dinner, for Paris' best ice cream, and for a stroll to Notre-Dame.

Get your Left Bank buzz in the area around Place St. Germain-des-Prés and Odéon (Mo: St. Germain-des-Prés and Odéon), full of famous cafés, cinemas, and night owls prowling along Rue des Canettes, Rue Guisarde, and Rue de Buci. Montmartre is touristy but lively, and a bit dicey at night. For old-time cabaret ambience, consider Au Lapin Agile (€35, shows in French only, tel. 01 46 06 85 87, http://aulapinagile.fr), and end the evening in front of Sacré-Cœur Basilica.

Sleeping

In Paris, choosing the right neighborhood is as important as choosing the right hotel. I've focused most of my recommendations in three safe, handy, and colorful neighborhoods: the village-like Rue Cler (near the Eiffel Tower), the artsy and trendy Marais (near Place de la Bastille), and the lively and classy Luxembourg (on the Left Bank). I also list a handful of places on Ile St. Louis, Rue Mouffetard, and in Montmartre. I like hotels that are clean, central, relatively quiet at night, reasonably priced, friendly, small enough to have a hands-on owner or manager, and run with a respect for French traditions.

Double rooms listed in this book average around €130-200 (with private bathrooms). They range from a low of roughly €70 (very simple; toilet and shower down the hall) to €400 (maximum plumbing and more).

Paris Hotels

Book any accommodations well in advance, especially if you'll be traveling during peak season or if your trip coincides with a major holiday. Within each hotel, prices vary depending on the size of room, whether it has a tub or shower, and the bed type (tubs and twins usually cost more than showers and double beds). If you'll take either twins or a double, ask for a generic *une chambre pour deux* (room for two).

Hotel elevators are common, though small, and some older buildings still lack them. Most hotel rooms have a TV and free Wi-Fi, which can vary in strength and quality.

Most hotels offer breakfast, but it's rarely included in the room rates (generally €10-20). It's usually a buffet breakfast (cereal, yogurt, fruit, cheese, ham, croissants, juice, and hard-boiled eggs). Coffee is often self-serve.

Note that the French hotel rating system (zero to five stars) reflects the number of amenities (e.g., fancier lobbies, more elaborately designed rooms), and does not necessarily rate quality.

Making Reservations

Reserve your rooms as soon as you've pinned down your travel dates. Book your room directly via email or phone or through the hotel's official website. The hotelier wants to know:

- Type(s) of room(s) you want and number of guests
- Number of nights you'll stay
- Arrival and departure dates, written European-style as day/month/year (for example, 18/06/24 or 18 June 2024)
- Special requests (en suite bathroom, cheapest room, twin beds vs. double bed, quiet room)
- Applicable discounts (such as a Rick Steves discount, cash discount, or promotional rate)

Most places will request a credit-card number to hold your room. If the hotel's website doesn't have a secure form where you can enter the number directly, share this info via a phone call.

If you must cancel, it's courteous—and smart—to do so with as much notice as possible. Cancellation policies can be strict; read the fine print. Always call or email to reconfirm your reservation a few days in advance. For *chambres d'hôtes* or very small hotels, I call again

Sleep Code

Dollar signs reflect average rates for a standard double room without breakfast in high season.

$$$$	**Splurge:** Most rooms over €300
$$$	**Pricier:** €200-300
$$	**Moderate:** €130-200
$	**Budget:** €70-130
¢	**Backpacker:** Under €70
RS%	**Rick Steves discount**
*	**French hotel rating system** (0-5 stars)

Unless otherwise noted, credit cards are accepted, hotel staff speak basic English, and free Wi-Fi is available. If the listing includes **RS%**, request a Rick Steves discount.

on my arrival day to tell my host what time to expect me (especially if arriving after 17:00).

Budget Tips

Comparison-shop by checking prices at several hotels (on each hotel's own website, on a booking site, or by email). For the best deal, *book directly with the hotel*. Ask for a discount if paying in cash.

For lower rates or greater selection, look farther from the river, but be prepared to spend more time getting to sights.

If you're staying in one place for several nights, it's worth considering an apartment—especially for groups and families. European apartments, like hotel rooms, tend to be small by US standards, but often come with laundry facilities and compact, equipped kitchens. Websites such as Airbnb, FlipKey, Booking.com, and VRBO let you browse properties and correspond directly with European property owners.

In Paris, you can also try Paris Perfect (English-speaking staff, RS%, www.parisperfect.com), Cobblestone Paris Rentals (rentals in central neighborhoods, RS%—use code "RSPARIS"—plus two free river cruises, www.cobblestoneparis.com), Home Rental Service (big selection with no agency fees, www.homerental.fr), Paris for Rent (top-end apartments, www.parisforrent.com), Adrian Leeds Group (longer-term rentals, https://adrianleeds.com), or Cross-Pollinate (reputable B&Bs and apartments, www.cross-pollinate.com).

SLEEPING

RUE CLER AREA

A safe, tidy, upscale area near the Eiffel Tower; Mo: Ecole Militaire, La Tour Maubourg, and Invalides

$$$$ Hôtel du Cadran**** A well-placed *boule* toss from Rue Cler, modern and *très* stylish, wine bar in lobby, designer rooms, RS% includes big breakfast—use code "RICK".
10 Rue du Champ de Mars, +33 1 40 62 67 00, www.cadranhotel.com

$$$ Hôtel Relais Bosquet*** A fine hotel in an ideal location, comfortable public spaces, well-configured rooms are large by local standards, RS%—use code "RSDEAL".
19 Rue du Champ de Mars, +33 1 47 05 25 45, www.hotel-paris-bosquet.com

$$$ Cler Hotel*** Eager-to-please boutique hotel with appealing decor, small outdoor patio, killer location right on Rue Cler, well-designed rooms, RS%.
24 bis Rue Cler, +33 1 45 00 18 06, www.clerhotel.com

$$$ Hôtel de la Motte Picquet*** At the corner of Rue Cler and Avenue de la Motte-Picquet, intimate and modest with 16 compact yet comfortable-enough rooms, terrific staff, good breakfast served in minuscule breakfast room, easy bike rental, family rooms, RS%—use code "STEVE-SMITH".
30 Avenue de la Motte-Picquet, +33 1 47 05 09 57, www.hotelmottepicquetparis.com

$$ Hôtel du Champ de Mars*** Top choice, brilliantly located just 30 yards off Rue Cler, adorable rooms are snug but lovingly kept by hands-on owner Céline, a few well-priced single rooms, continental breakfast only.
7 Rue du Champ de Mars, +33 1 45 51 52 30, www.hotelduchampdemars.com

$$ Hôtel Beaugency*** Thirty smallish rooms, most with double beds, lobby that you can stretch out in, fair value on a quieter street, free breakfast for Rick Steves readers.
21 Rue Duvivier, +33 1 47 05 01 63, www.hotel-beaugency.com

$$$ Hôtel de Londres Eiffel**** My closest listing to the Eiffel Tower and the Champ de Mars park, immaculate and warmly decorated rooms, welcoming public spaces, terrific staff, family rooms, RS%.
1 Rue Augereau, +33 1 45 51 63 02, www.londres-eiffel.com

$ Hôtel de la Tour Eiffel** Solid budget value on a quiet street, rooms are simple but well designed and with air-conditioning, connecting rooms are ideal for families, RS%.
17 Rue de l'Exposition, +33 1 47 05 14 75, www.hotel-toureiffel.com

$ Hôtel Kensington** Fair budget value close to the Eiffel Tower, unpretentious place offering basic comfort, some partial Eiffel Tower views, no air-con but ceiling fans.
79 Avenue de la Bourdonnais, +33 1 47 05 74 00, www.hotel-eiffel-kensington.com

$$$$ Hôtel de Latour-Maubourg**** Peaceful manor-home setting, 17 plush and mostly large rooms, small patio, free spa for clients.

150 Rue de Grenelle, +33 1 47 05 16 16, www.latourmaubourg.com

$$$ Hôtel les Jardins d'Eiffel*** Big place on a quiet street, impersonal service, peaceful patio, 81 well-configured rooms—some with partial Eiffel Tower views, some with balconies.

8 Rue Amélie, +33 1 47 05 46 21, www.hoteljardinseiffel.com

$$$ Hôtel de l'Empereur*** Plush, delivers smashing views of Invalides from many of its fine rooms, all rooms have queen- or king-size beds and are large by Paris standards, some view rooms, family rooms.

2 Rue Chevert, +33 1 45 55 88 02, www.hotelempereurparis.com

$$$ Hôtel Muguet*** Quiet, well located, and reasonable, tastefully appointed rooms, helpful staff, some view rooms.

11 Rue Chevert, +33 1 47 05 05 93, www.hotelparismuguet.com

$$$ Hôtel Eiffel Turenne*** Sharp, well-maintained rooms, pleasing lounge, service-oriented staff.

20 Avenue de Tourville, +33 1 47 05 99 92, www.hoteleiffelturenne.com

$$$ Hôtel de la Paix*** Intimate place buried on a quiet lane, tastefully designed rooms, six true singles, free breakfast for Rick Steves readers who book direct.

19 Rue du Gros Caillou, +33 1 45 51 86 17, https://hotelparispaix.com

$$ Hôtel Duquesne Eiffel*** Handsome and hospitable, reasonably priced, welcoming lobby, street-front terrace, comfortable rooms (some with terrific Eiffel Tower views), family rooms, RS%, free breakfast for my readers.

23 Avenue Duquesne, +33 1 44 42 09 09, www.hotel-duquesne-eiffel-paris.com

MARAIS AREA

Classy mansions alongside trendy boutiques create a Greenwich Village vibe; Mo: Bastille, St-Paul, and Hôtel de Ville

$$$ Hôtel Bastille Spéria*** Situated a short block off Place de la Bastille, business-type service and good comfort, happening location, 42 rooms with designer decor, relatively spacious.

1 Rue de la Bastille, +33 1 42 72 04 01, www.hotelsperia.com

$$$ Hôtel St. Louis Marais*** Intimate and sharp little hotel, on a quiet street a few blocks from the river, handsome rooms have character and spacious bathrooms.

1 Rue Charles V, Mo: Sully-Morland, +33 1 48 87 87 04, www.saintlouismarais.com

$$$ Hôtel Castex*** Well-located place on a quiet street near Place de la Bastille, narrow and tile-floored rooms, connecting rooms for families, free buffet breakfast for Rick Steves readers, just off Place de la Bastille and Rue St. Antoine.

5 Rue Castex, +33 1 42 72 31 52, www.castexhotel.com

$$ Hôtel Jeanne d'Arc*** Lovely hotel, ideally located, artful decor of stone walls and oak floors, thoughtfully appointed rooms, corner rooms are wonderfully bright, rooms on the street can have some noise, family rooms, some view rooms, no air-con.

3 Rue de Jarente, +33 1 48 87 62 11, www.hoteljeannedarc.com

$$ Hôtel de Neuve*** Small, central, and unpretentious place, rooms are pleasant, quiet, and a good value in this pricey area, twin rooms come with tub-showers and are a bit larger.

14 Rue de Neuve, +33 1 44 59 28 50, www.hoteldeneuveparis.com.

$ Sully Hôtel* Basic and cheap place, rooms are simple but updated, good budget value, two can spring for a triple for more room, family rooms, no elevator, no air-con, no breakfast.

48 Rue St. Antoine, +33 1 42 78 49 32, www.sullyhotelparis.com

¢ MIJE Fourcy Classy, old residence-turned-hostel, ideal for budget travelers, dirt-cheap dinners available with a membership card, no air-con.

6 Rue de Fourcy, just south of Rue de Rivoli, +33 1 42 74 23 45, www.mije.com

¢ MIJE Fauconnier Sibling hostel with same contact info as MIJE Fourcy, no elevator.

11 Rue du Fauconnier

$$ Hôtel de la Bretonnerie*** Three blocks from the Hôtel de Ville, warm and welcoming lobby, helpful staff, 30 good-value rooms on the larger side, family rooms, free breakfast for Rick Steves readers who book direct, no air-con, between Rue Vieille du Temple and Rue des Archives.

22 Rue Ste. Croix de la Bretonnerie, +33 1 48 87 77 63,
www.hotelparismaraisbretonnerie.com

$$ Hôtel Beaubourg*** Top value on a small street in the shadow of the Pompidou Center, surprisingly quiet, 28 plush and traditional rooms, bigger doubles worth the extra cost.

11 Rue Simon Le Franc, Mo: Rambuteau, +33 1 42 74 34 24, www.hotelbeaubourg.com

ILE ST. LOUIS AREA

Island in the Seine near Notre-Dame: peaceful, residential, and pricey; Mo: Pont Marie and Sully-Morland

$$$ Hôtel de Lutèce* ** Welcoming wood-paneled lobby, traditional and warm rooms—most with wood-beam ceilings, rooms on lower floors have high ceilings, rooms with bathtubs are streetside, those with showers are on the quieter courtyard.

65 Rue St. Louis-en-l'Ile, +33 1 43 26 23 52, www.hoteldelutece.com

$$$ Hôtel des Deux-Iles* ** Lovely rooms, a few true singles, a bit cheaper than the Lutèce but otherwise hard to distinguish—you can't go wrong in either place.

59 Rue St. Louis-en-l'Ile, +33 1 43 26 13 35, www.hoteldesdeuxiles.com

$$$ Hôtel Saint-Louis* ** Sharp rooms blend character with modern comforts, stone floors and exposed beams, rates are reasonable for the location.

75 Rue St. Louis-en-l'Ile, +33 1 46 34 04 80, www.saintlouisenlisle.com

LUXEMBOURG GARDEN AREA

Left Bank energy with shops, cafés, and the park; Mo: Cluny-La Sorbonne, St. Sulpice, Mabillon, and Odéon

$$$$ Hôtel de l'Abbaye** ** Lovely refuge just west of Luxembourg Garden, four-star luxury, refined lounges inside and out, 44 sumptuous rooms with every amenity.

10 Rue Cassette, +33 1 45 44 38 11, www.hotelabbayeparis.com

$$$$ Hôtel le Récamier** ** Romantically tucked in the corner of Place St. Sulpice, designer public spaces, elaborately appointed rooms, courtyard tea salon, complimentary tea and treats in the afternoon, top-notch professional service, connecting family rooms.

3 bis Place St. Sulpice, +33 1 43 26 04 89, www.hotelrecamier.com

$$$ Hôtel Relais St. Sulpice* ** Burrowed on the small street just behind St. Sulpice Church, cozy lounge, 26 artsy rooms—most surrounding a leafy glass atrium, street-facing rooms get more light, those on the courtyard are quieter, sauna free for guests.

3 Rue Garancière, +33 1 46 33 99 00, www.relais-saint-sulpice.com

$$$ Hôtel la Perle* ** In the thick of lively Rue des Canettes, a block off Place St. Sulpice, well-run hotel built around a central bar and atrium, comfortable and traditional rooms.

14 Rue des Canettes, +33 1 43 29 10 10, www.hotellaperle.com

$$ Hôtel Bonaparte* ** Unpretentious and welcoming place wedged between boutiques, a few steps from Place St. Sulpice, decor is simple, rooms are spacious, staff is very helpful.

61 Rue Bonaparte, +33 1 43 26 97 37, www.hotelbonaparte.fr

SLEEPING

$$$ Hôtel Signature St. Germain-des-Prés**** On a quiet street just steps from the trendy Sèvres-Babylone shopping area, feels as chic as its neighboring boutiques, friendly staff, 26 colorful and tastefully decorated rooms—several with balconies, family rooms, RS%.

5 Rue Chomel, Mo: Sèvres-Babylone, +33 1 45 48 35 53, www.signature-saintgermain.com

$$$ Hôtel le Petit Chomel*** Great location, good rates, comfortable rooms, warm public spaces, helpful staff, decor with a country-French accent, RS%.

15 Rue Chomel, +33 1 45 48 55 52, www.lepetitchomel.com

$ Hôtel Jean Bart** A rare budget find in this neighborhood, one block from Luxembourg Garden, dark lobby, 33 suitably comfortable rooms with creaking floors—some with tight bathrooms, includes breakfast, no air-con.

9 Rue Jean-Bart, +33 1 45 48 29 13, www.hoteljeanbart.com

$$$ Hôtel Victoire et Germain**** Top choice a few steps off Boulevard St. Germain and Rue de Buci, excellent comfort, Scandinavian accents under white beams.

9 Rue Grégoire de Tours, +33 1 45 49 03 26, www.victoireetgermainhotel.com

$$$ Hôtel Relais Médicis**** Ideal if you've always wanted to live in a Monet painting, glassy entry hides 17 rooms surrounding a fragrant little garden courtyard and fountain, tastefully decorated, permeated with thoughtfulness, family rooms, faces the Odéon Theater.

5 Place de l'Odéon, +33 1 43 26 00 60, www.relaismedicis.com

$$$ Hôtel des Marronniers*** Wonderfully situated on a quiet street, delivers Old World charm with modern comfort, atrium breakfast room, lovely garden courtyard, cozy lounges, plush rooms.
21 Rue Jacob, +33 1 43 25 30 60, *www.hotel-marronniers.com*

$$$ Odéon Hôtel*** Large lobby-lounge, dark hallways, Old World-style rooms with all the comforts.

3 Rue de l'Odéon, + 33 1 43 25 90 76, www.odeonhotel.fr

$$ Hôtel Michelet Odéon** In a corner of Place de l'Odéon with big windows overlooking the square, rooms come with stylish colors but no frills, impersonal staff, family rooms, no air-con.
6 Place de l'Odéon, +33 1 53 10 05 60, *www.hotelmicheletodeon.com*

$$$ Hôtel des Grandes Ecoles*** Idyllic place, flower-filled garden courtyard, 51 rooms are French-countryside pretty, reasonably spacious, lovingly cared for, no TVs, reserve ahead for pay parking.

75 Rue du Cardinal Lemoine, Mo: Cardinal Lemoine, +33 1 43 26 79 23, www.hoteldesgrandesecoles.com

MONTMARTRE AREA

Lively, untouristy base of the hill, great for young and budget travelers; Mo: Abbesses, Anvers, Blanche, and Pigalle

$$$ Le Relais Montmartre* Spotless hotel with cushy public spaces, 26 cozy rooms sporting floral curtains, lots of amenities including shared iPad, fireplace, quiet central courtyard.

6 Rue Constance, +33 1 70 64 25 25, www.hotel-relais-montmartre.com

$$$ Hôtel Littéraire Marcel Aymé* Stylish and somewhat pricey, a few blocks below the Moulin de la Galette, smallish but well-designed rooms.

16 Rue Tholozé, +33 1 42 55 05 06, www.hotel-litteraire-marcel-ayme.com

$$ Timhotel Montmartre On a small leafy square, short walk from the top of the hill, next to famous Bateau-Lavoir artists' hangout, rooms are handsome and well maintained—and a fair value, rooms on the fourth and fifth floors have city views.

11 Rue Ravignan, +33 1 42 55 74 79, www.timhotel.com

$ Hôtel Regyn's Montmartre Welcoming and ideally located on the lively Abbesses square, 22 comfortable rooms with floral wallpaper, some with pleasant views and noise from the square, other rooms with grand views to the Eiffel Tower, no air-con, great breakfast.

18 Place des Abbesses, +33 1 42 54 45 21, www.regyns-montmartre.com

$ Hôtel Audran A few stops off Rue des Abbesses, fair budget value, 39 simple rooms, some fourth- and fifth-floor rooms come with views.

7 Rue Audran, +33 1 42 58 79 59, www.hotelaudran.com

$ Hôtel Bonséjour Montmartre Mix of modern and basic rooms, modern rooms have private bathrooms and new beds, cheaper ones have shared facilities—one shower for every two rooms, run by eager Michel and his family, RS%, no air-con.

11 Rue Burq, +33 1 42 54 22 53, www.hotel-bonsejour.com

SLEEPING

Eating

The Parisian eating scene is kept at a rolling boil. Entire books (and lives) are dedicated to the subject, and trendy chefs are stalked by the paparazzi. Parisians eat long and well. Relaxed lunches, three-hour dinners, and endless hours of sitting in outdoor cafés are the norm. Budget some money—and time—to sightseeing for your palate. Even if the rest of you is sleeping in a cheap hotel, let your taste buds travel first-class in Paris.

I list a full range of restaurants and eateries, from budget options for a quick bite to multicourse splurges with maximum ambience. My listings are in Paris' atmospheric neighborhoods, handy to recommended hotels and sights.

When in Paris...

I eat on the Parisian schedule. For breakfast, I eat at the hotel or belly up to a café counter for a quick café au lait and croissant. Lunch (12:00-14:30) may be a big salad or *plat du jour,* or an atmospheric picnic. In the late afternoon, Parisians enjoy a beverage at a sidewalk table. Dinner is the time for slowing down and savoring a multicourse restaurant meal.

Restaurants

French restaurants open for dinner around 19:00 (some at 18:30) and can be packed by 21:00. Many restaurants close Sunday and/or Monday. All café and restaurant interiors are smoke-free, but outdoor tables can be smoky.

A full restaurant meal comes in courses. It might include an *aperitif* (before-dinner drink), an *entrée* (starter course/appetizer), a *plat principal* (main dish), cheese course, dessert, coffee, liqueurs, several different wines, and so on. You can choose something off the menu (*la carte*), or you can order a multicourse, fixed-price meal (confusingly, called a *menu*). Or, if offered, you can get one of the special dishes of the day (*plat du jour*). If you ask for *un menu* (instead of *la carte*), you'll get a fixed-price meal.

It's not obligatory to order every course—in fact, many Parisians consider two courses (e.g., *plat* and dessert) a "full" meal. Ordering as little as a single main dish as your entire meal is acceptable. Two people can split an *entrée* or a big salad (small-size dinner salads are usually not offered á la carte) and then each get a *plat principal*. If all you want is a salad or soup, go to a café or brasserie.

Most restaurants offer less expensive and less filling two-course *menus,* sometimes called *formules,* featuring an *entrée et plat,* or *plat et dessert.* Wine and other drinks are extra, and certain premium items add a few euros, clearly noted on the menu (*supplément* or *sup.*). Parisians are willing to pay for bottled water with their meal (*eau minérale*), but a free carafe of tap water (*une carafe d'eau*) is always available upon request. Regardless of what you order, bread is free.

At cafés and restaurants, a service charge is included in the price of what you order, and it's unnecessary to tip extra, though you can for helpful service. French servers probably won't overwhelm you with friendliness.

To get a server's attention, try to make meaningful eye contact,

Restaurant Code

Dollar signs reflect the cost of a typical main course.

$$$$	**Splurge:** Most main courses over €40
$$$	**Pricier:** €30-40
$$	**Moderate:** €20-30
$	**Budget:** Under €20

A crêpe stand or other takeout spot is $; a sit-down brasserie, café, or bistro with affordable *plats du jour* ranges from $ to $$; a casual but more upscale restaurant is $$$; and a swanky splurge is $$$$.

raise your hand, and say, *"S'il vous plaît"*—"please." This phrase also works when asking for the check—*"L'addition, s'il vous plaît."* The server will rarely bring you the check unless you request it. To the French, having the bill dropped off before asking for it is *gauche*.

To get the most out of dining out in France, slow down. Give yourself time to dine at a French pace, engage the waitstaff, show you care about food, and enjoy the experience as much as the food itself. *Bon appétit.*

Cafés and Brasseries

Less formal than restaurants, these places serve user-friendly meals, as well as coffee and drinks. They serve food throughout the day, and you're welcome to order just a salad, a sandwich, or a bowl of soup (even for dinner). It's also OK to share starters and desserts, though not main courses.

Feel free to order a *plat* (main course), a *plat du jour* (daily special), a salad (they're usually big), a sandwich (e.g. a *croque monsieur*, or grilled ham and cheese sandwich), an omelet, an *entrée* (appetizer), or a bowl of soup. Many cafés and brasseries have outdoor tables (with braziers in winter), perfect for nursing a glass of wine or café au lait, and watching the parade of passersby. A *crêperie*—serving both sweet dessert crêpes and meal-like savory ones—is another less formal, budget alternative.

There are two sets of prices: You'll pay more for the same drink if you're seated at a table (*salle*) than if you're seated or standing at the bar or counter (*comptoir*).

Enjoy a streetside café...   ...or a riverfront picnic.

Picnicking

Paris makes it easy to turn a picnic into a first-class affair. Takeout delis (a *charcuterie* or *traiteur,* as well as some bakeries) sell high-quality cooked dishes, quiches, pâtés, small pizzas, and salads you can build a meal around. The deli can warm it up for you (*chauffé* = heated up) and pack it in a takeout box (*une barquette*), along with a plastic fork (*fourchette*).

For side dishes, a generic *supermarché* is easy for one-stop shopping, but you'll do better browsing a *boulangerie* for your baguette, a *fromagerie* for cheese, and an open-air market for the freshest produce.

Be daring. Try the smelly cheeses, strange-looking pâtés, and minuscule yogurts. Some good picnic spots in the heart of Paris are the Palais Royal courtyard, the Place des Vosges, the west tip of Ile de la Cité, and the Tuileries Garden.

French Cuisine

You can be a galloping gourmet and try several types of French cuisine without ever leaving the confines of Paris. Most restaurants serve dishes from several regions, though some focus on a particular region's cuisine.

From Burgundy (among France's best cuisines), try *coq au vin* (rooster with red wine sauce), *bœuf bourguignon* (beef stew), or *escargots*. From Normandy and Brittany you'll find mussels and oysters, crêpes, and cider. Any dish prepared *à la provençale* features that region's garlic, olive oil, herbs, and tomatoes. You'll find bouillabaisse from the Côte d'Azur, *pâté de foie gras* (goose-liver pâté) from the southwest, and even Alsatian *choucroute*—sauerkraut.

Paris has a particular fondness for steak, including *steak tartare*—raw ground beef. Duck from the Dordogne region (*confit de canard*), leg of lamb (*gigot d'agneau*), roasted chicken (*poulet roti*), and salmon (*saumon*) are also popular. Raw oysters (*huîtres*) from Brittany are a Christmas tradition. Sauces are a huge part of French cooking. The five classics are *béchamel* (milk-based white sauce), *espagnole* (veal-based brown sauce), *velouté* (stock-based white sauce), *tomate* (tomato-based red sauce), and *hollandaise* (egg yolk-based white sauce).

Commonly served cheeses are Brie de Meaux (mild and creamy, from just outside Paris), Camembert (semicreamy and pungent, from Normandy), *chèvre* (goat cheese with a sharp taste, from the Loire), and Roquefort (strong and blue-veined, from south-central France). Many restaurants will bring you a variety platter from which you can choose.

For dessert, try a *café gourmand*, an assortment of small desserts selected by the restaurant. Other classic desserts include *crème bruleé*, *tarte tatin*, and *mousse au chocolat*.

No meal in France is complete without wine. Even the basic table wine (*vin du pays*) is fine with a meal—order it by the pitcher, or *pichet*. For good-but-inexpensive wines by the bottle, look for reds from Côtes du Rhone or Languedoc, and whites from Burgundy or Alsace. In summer, everyone should try an inexpensive rosé. Those willing to pay more can get a good (but not cheap) pinot noir from Burgundy, or a heavier red from Bordeaux.

The French don't drink wine as an apéritif. More common are champagne, beer, a Kir (a dash of *crème de cassis* with white wine), or Pastis (an anise-flavored liquor from Provence). France's best beer is Alsatian; try Kronenbourg or the heavier Pelfort. *Une panaché* is a refreshing French shandy (lemon soda and beer).

For coffee, Parisians like *un café* (shot of espresso), a café au lait/ *café crème* (espresso with lots of steamed milk), or *une noisette* (espresso with a shot of milk). A fun, bright, nonalcoholic drink is un *diabolo menthe*, featuring 7-Up with mint syrup. If you're ordering a Coke, remember that Paris' last ice cubes melted after the last Yankee tour group left.

RUE CLER AREA

Eateries catering to upscale residents near the Eiffel Tower, Mo: Ecole Militaire, La Tour-Maubourg, or Bastille (see map, page 206)

❶ $ Café du Marché Best seats on Rue Cler, inexpensive one-course meals, hearty salads, filling *plats du jour*, often packed after 19:00 (daily).

38 Rue Cler, +33 1 47 05 51 27

❷ $ Le Petit Cler Popular little bistro, long leather booths, vintage interior, tiny and cramped tables—indoors and out, inexpensive *plats* (daily).

29 Rue Cler, +33 1 45 50 17 50

❸ $$ Le Septième Vin Cozy and welcoming, delicious traditional cuisine, good prices, romantic and very Parisian setting (closed Sun).

68 Avenue Bosquet, +33 1 45 51 15 97

❹ $$$ Le Florimond Warm setting, classic French cuisine at fair prices, one small room of tables; tasty stuffed cabbage, lobster ravioli, and *confit de canard;* friendly Laurent and chef Pascale (closed Sat-Sun, reservations smart).

19 Avenue de la Motte-Picquet, +33 1 45 55 40 38, www.leflorimond.com

❺ $$$ Bistrot Belhara Vintage French dining, intimate space, inventive and classic dishes, good-value *menu* (closed Sun-Mon, reservations smart).

23 Rue Duvivier, +33 1 45 51 41 77, www.bistrotbelhara.com

❻ $$ Café le Bosquet Contemporary brasserie, decent prices inside or outside on a broad sidewalk; standard café fare—salad, French onion soup, *steak-frites,* or a *plat du jour* (closed Sun).

46 Avenue Bosquet, +33 1 45 51 38 13, www.bosquetparis.com

❼ $$ La Terrasse du 7ème Sprawling and happening café, grand outdoor seating, living room-like interior with comfy love seats, good salads, French onion soup, and foie gras (daily until 24:00).

2 Place de L'Ecole Militaire, +33 1 45 55 00 02

❽ $$$ Au Petit Tonneau Endearing French bistro, time-warp decor, fleur-de-lis tiled floor, carefully prepared food but limited menu, away from Rue Cler tourist crush, good à la carte choices or three-course *menu* that changes with the season, well-priced wines, charming owner Arlette (closed Mon off-season).

20 Rue Surcouf, +33 1 47 05 09 01

❾ $$ Le P'tit Troquet Petite eatery, recalls 1920s Paris, tasty range of traditional choices, homey charm, tight little dining room, €40 three-course dinner *menu* (closed Sun, reservations smart).

28 Rue de l'Exposition, +33 1 47 05 80 39, www.leptittroquet.fr

⑩ **$$ Café de Mars** Relaxed place, creative cuisine draws from many countries, good vegetarian options, fair prices, welcoming counter (closed Sun-Mon).

11 Rue Augereau, +33 1 45 50 10 90

⑪ **$ Le Royal** Tiny neighborhood fixture, simple traditional dishes, prices and decor from another era (closed Sun).

212 Rue de Grenelle, +33 1 47 53 92 90

⑫ **$$$ La Fontaine de Mars** Neighborhood institution, on a tiny and jumbled square, superb foie gras and desserts (daily, reserve in advance for a table on the ground floor or square).

129 Rue St. Dominique, +33 1 47 05 46 44, www.fontainedemars.com

⑬ **$$$$ Le Violon d'Ingres** Michelin star restaurant, fine dining in a serious but accessible eating scene, order à la carte or get the €150 seven-course tasting *menu,* cheaper at lunch (daily, reservations essential).

135 Rue St. Dominique, +33 1 45 55 15 05, www.maisonconstant.com

⑭ **$ Crep' and Tea** Creative menu of homemade crêpes, tidy shoebox-size room with Tetris seating (daily).

139 Rue St. Dominique, +33 1 45 51 70 78

MARAIS AREA

Trendy places amid boisterous nightlife, Mo: St-Paul, Bastille, Chemin Vert, or Hôtel de Ville (see map, page 208)

⑮ **$$ La Place Royale** Traditional menu, exceptional location on romantic Place des Vosges, comfortable seating, good for a relaxed lunch or dinner, well-priced hearty cuisine, lengthy wine list (daily, reserve ahead to dine outside).

2 bis Place des Vosges, +33 1 42 78 58 16

⑯ **$ Café Hugo** Salads and basic café fare, Parisian energy, food is just OK but the setting is terrific, good seating under the arches (daily).

22 Place des Vosges, +33 1 42 72 64 04

⑰ **$$ Chez Janou** Provençal bistro, fills the sidewalk with happy eaters, helpful and patient service, French Mediterranean with an emphasis on vegetables (daily, book ahead or arrive when it opens at 19:00).

2 Rue Roger Verlomme, +33 1 42 72 28 41, www.chezjanou.com

⑱ **$$ Le Petit Marché** Warm bistro, friendly service, tasty cuisine blending French classics with an Asian influence (daily, smart to book a day ahead).

9 Rue du Béarn, +33 1 42 72 06 67, www.lepetitmarche.eu

⑲ **$$ Brasserie Bofinger** Famous for seafood and traditional cuisine with Alsatian flair, sprawling interior, one-of-a-kind ambience, reminiscent of the Roaring Twenties (daily for lunch and dinner).

5 Rue de la Bastille, +33 1 42 72 87 82, www.bofingerparis.com

⑳ **$$ Le Temps des Cerises** Warm place with wads of character, young and lively vibe, tight inside seating, a few outdoor tables, tasty dinners with generous portions (daily).

31 Rue de la Cerisaie, +33 1 42 72 08 63

㉑ **$$ Le Marché** Fun, cheap place on Place du Marché Ste. Catherine—the Marais' most romantic square, tight seating on simple chairs indoors and out, cheaper for lunch (daily).

2 Place du Marché Ste. Catherine, +33 01 40 09 05 33

㉒ **$$ Chez Marianne** Neighborhood fixture, tasty Jewish cuisine, fun atmosphere with Parisian *élan,* sit outside or indoors with a cluttered wine shop/deli feeling, great vegetarian options (long hours daily).

2 Rue des Hospitalières St. Gervais—at the corner with Rue des Rosiers, +33 1 42 72 18 86

㉓ **$$ Le Loir dans la Théière** Cozy and mellow teahouse, welcoming ambience, daily assortment of creative quiches, homemade desserts (daily 9:00-19:00, only dessert-type items after 15:00).

3 Rue des Rosiers, +33 1 42 72 90 61

㉔ **$$$ Au Bourguignon du Marais** Dressy wine bar/bistro for Burgundy lovers, excellent wines by the glass, well-designed dishes, efficient service (daily).

52 Rue François Miron, +33 1 48 87 15 40

㉕ **$ L'Ebouillanté** Breezy café a block off the river, good for an inexpensive and relaxing tea, snack, lunch, or dinner on a warm evening (daily 12:00-21:30, closes earlier in winter).

6 Rue des Barres, +33 1 42 74 70 52

㉖ **$$ Au Petit Fer à Cheval** Fairly priced, horseshoe-shaped zinc bar immerses you in the clatter of the scene, tight dining room in the rear is Old World adorable, outdoor tables are street-theater perfect (daily).

30 Rue Vieille du Temple, +33 1 42 72 47 47

ILE ST. LOUIS

Quiet, romantic area perfect for after-dinner strolling, Mo: Pont Marie (see map, page 208)

㉗ **$$ Nos Ancêtres les Gaulois** Famously rowdy, medieval-cellar atmosphere, all-you-can-eat for €40 (daily).

39 Rue St. Louis-en-l'Ile, +33 1 46 33 66 07

㉘ **$$ Les Fous de l'Ile** Fun place, bistro fare with gourmet touches for a good price, 2- or 3-course *menus* or *plat du jour* only (daily).

33 Rue des Deux Ponts, +33 1 43 25 76 67

㉙ **$$ L'Orangerie** Inviting, rustic yet elegant, comfortable seating, hushed ambience, cuisine blends traditional with modern touches (closed Mon).

28 Rue St. Louis-en-l'Ile, +33 1 85 15 21 31

㉚ **$ Auberge de la Reine Blanche** Woodsy and cozy, rub elbows with your neighbors, basic French cuisine at reasonable prices, good dinner salads, earnest owner Michel (opens at 18:30, closed Mon).

30 Rue St. Louis-en-l'Ile, +33 1 85 15 21 30

㉛ **On Ile de la Cité: $$ Les Deux Palais** Venerable old-school bistro, 1870s ambience, professional service, decent prices, convenient location facing Sainte-Chapelle, handy for lunch or a drink while sightseeing (daily until 21:00).

3 Boulevard du Palais, +33 1 34 54 20 86

LUXEMBOURG GARDEN AREA

Lively near St. Sulpice, quieter near Panthéon, Mo: St-Sulpice or St-German-des-Près (see map, page 208)

㉜ **$$ Monte Verdi** Italian cuisine served in several rooms, live piano music, each room offers a different experience (closed Sun).

5 Rue Guisarde, +33 1 42 34 55 90, www.lemonteverdi.com

㉝ **$$$ Chez Fernand** Solid choice, great range of classic and beefy bistro fare, tight seating, red-checkered tablecloths, high-energy immersion in French dining (opens at 19:00, closed Mon).

13 Rue Guisarde, +33 1 43 54 61 47

㉞ **$$$$ La Méditerranée** Seafood from the south, pastel setting, formal yet accessible, *formidable* view of the Odéon (daily from 19:30, reservations smart).

2 Place de l'Odéon, +33 1 43 26 02 30, www.la-mediterranee.com

㉟ **$ Restaurant Polidor** Parisian equivalent of a beloved neighborhood diner, fixture since 1845, lively old-Paris atmosphere, shared tables, classic dishes from every corner of France (daily, reservations smart).

41 Rue Monsieur-le-Prince, +33 1 43 26 95 34, www.polidor.com

㊱ **$$$ Les Deux Magots** and **㊲** **Café de Flore** Two famous cafés on a famous boulevard with a famous clientele.

Les Deux Magots—6 Place St. Germain-des-Prés, +33 1 45 48 55 25

Café de Flore—172 Boulevard St. Germain-des-Prés, +33 1 45 48 55 26

Rue Cler Area Restaurants

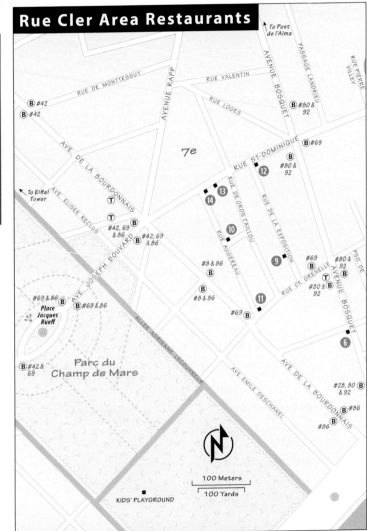

To Pont de l'Alma

RUE DE MONTTESSUY

AVENUE RAPP

RUE VALENTIN

AVENUE BOSQUET

PASSAGE LANDRIEU

RUE PIERRE VILLEY

Ⓑ #42
Ⓑ #42

RUE LOGES

Ⓑ #80 & 92

AVE. DE LA BOURDONNAIS

7e

RUE ST-DOMINIQUE

Ⓑ #69

Ⓑ #80 & 92

To Eiffel Tower

AVE. ELISEE RECLUS

Ⓣ

⑫

⑬
⑭

RUE DE GROS CAILLOU

RUE DE LA EXPOSITION

Ⓣ
Ⓑ #42, 69 & 86

Ⓑ #42, 69 & 86

⑩

RUE AUGEREAU

AVE. JOSEPH BOUVARD

Ⓑ #8 & 86

⑨

#69

Ⓑ #80 & 92

PSG. DE

Ⓑ #69 & 86
Ⓑ #69 & 86

Place Jacques Rueff

Ⓑ #8 & 86

⑪

RUE DE GRENELLE

Ⓣ
Ⓑ #80 & 92

AVENUE BOSQUET

Ⓑ #69

ALLEE ADRIENNE LECOUVREUR

Ⓑ #42 & 69

Parc du Champ de Mars

⑥

AVE. DE LA BOURDONNAIS

AVE. EMILE DESCHANEL

#28, 80 & 92 Ⓑ

Ⓑ #86

#86

N

100 Meters
100 Yards

KIDS' PLAYGROUND

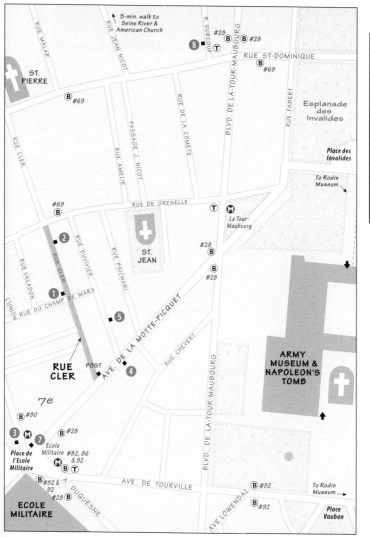

RUE MALAR

5-min. walk to Seine River & American Church

RUE JEAN NICOT

RUE SURCOUF

#28 B B #28

8

T

RUE ST-DOMINIQUE

B #69

ST. PIERRE

B #69

BLVD. DE-LA-TOUR-MAUBOURG

RUE FABERT

Esplanade des Invalides

RUE CLER

PASSAGE J. NICOT

RUE AMÉLIE

RUE DE LA COMÈTE

Place des Invalides

To Rodin Museum

#69 B

RUE DE GRENELLE

T

M La Tour-Maubourg

RUE VALADON

RUE CLER

2

RUE DUVIVIER

RUE PSICHARI

ST. JEAN

#28 B

B #28

L'UNION

1

RUE DU CHAMP DE MARS

5

AVE. DE LA MOTTE-PICQUET

RUE CHEVERT

RUE CLER

POST

4

ARMY MUSEUM & NAPOLEON'S TOMB

7e

BLVD. DE-LA-TOUR-MAUBOURG

B #80

3 M 7

B #28

Place de l'École Militaire

École Militaire #82, 86 & 92

M T

AVE. DE TOURVILLE

B #92

To Rodin Museum

ECOLE MILITAIRE

B #82 & 92

B #28

AVE. DUQUESNE

AVE. LOWENDAL

B #92

Place Vauban

Marais, Ile St. Louis & Luxembourg Garden Restaurants

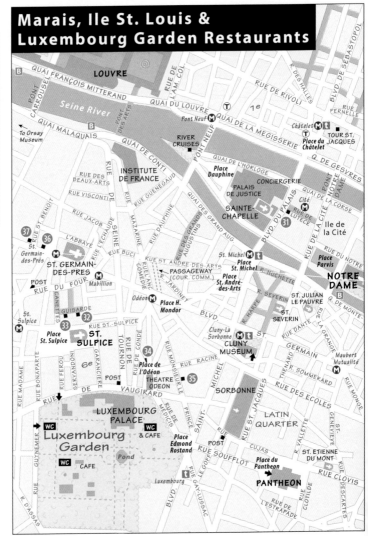

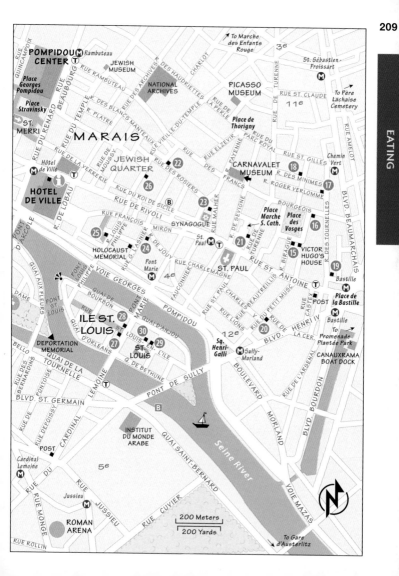

Practicalities

Travel Tips

Travel Advisories: Before traveling, check updated health and safety conditions, including restrictions for your destination, on the travel pages of the US State Department (www.travel.state.gov) and Centers for Disease Control and Prevention (www.cdc.gov/travel).

Tourist Information: Paris' tourist offices (abbreviated as "TI" in this book, www.parisinfo.com) can provide useful information. They sell Museum Passes and individual tickets to sights but charge a small fee—and may have longer lines than the museums. TIs also sell tickets to local concerts and events. The main TI is located at the **Hôtel de Ville** (daily 10:00-18:00, 29 Rue de Rivoli, on the north side of the building). Both **airports** have handy TIs with long hours.

Hurdling the Language Barrier: Most Parisians speak some English—certainly more English than Americans speak French. Still, learn the pleasantries, like *bonjour* (good day), *pardon* (pardon me), *s'il vous plaît* (please), *merci* (thank you), and *au revoir* (goodbye). Begin every encounter with *"Bonjour, madame* (or *monsieur),"* and end every encounter with *"Au revoir, madame* (or *monsieur)."*

Time Zones: France is six/nine hours ahead of the East/West Coasts of the US. For a handy time converter, use the world clock app on your phone or download one (see www.timeanddate.com).

Business Hours: Most smaller shops are open Monday through Saturday (10:00-12:00 & 14:00-19:00) and closed Sunday. These exceptions are open daily: large grocery stores, the Galeries Lafayette store near the Opéra Garnier, the Carrousel du Louvre underground shopping mall at the Louvre, and some shops near Sèvres-Babylone, along the Champs-Elysées, and in the Marais. Many small markets, *boulangeries* (bakeries), and street markets are open Sunday mornings until noon.

Watt's Up? Europe's electrical system is 220 volts, instead of North America's 110 volts. Most electronics (laptops, phones, cameras) and appliances (newer hair dryers, CPAP machines) convert automatically, so you won't need a converter, but you will need an adapter plug with two round prongs, sold inexpensively at travel stores in the US.

Helpful Websites

Paris' Tourist Information: ParisInfo.com

France's Tourist Information: Us.france.fr

Passports and Red Tape: Travel.state.gov

Cheap Flights: Kayak.com (for international flights), Skyscanner.com (for flights within Europe)

Airline Carry-on Restrictions: TSA.gov

European Train Schedules: Bahn.com

General Travel Tips: RickSteves.com (train travel, rail passes, car rental, travel insurance, packing lists, and much more)

Safety and Emergencies

Emergency and Medical Help: For any emergency service—ambulance, police, or fire—call **112** from a mobile phone or landline. If you get sick, do as the French do and go to a pharmacist for advice. Or ask at your hotel for help—they'll know the nearest medical and emergency services.

These places have English-speaking staff—**American Hospital** (63 Boulevard Victor Hugo, +33 1 46 41 25 25, www.american-hospital.org); **Pharmacie des Champs** (84 Avenue des Champs-Elysées, Mo: George V, +33 1 45 62 02 41); and **Pharmacie Anglaise** (62 Avenue des Champs-Elysées, +33 1 43 59 82 30). A list of **English-speaking doctors** is available on the US embassy's website: France.embassy.gov.au/pari/Engdoc.html.

Theft or Loss: Paris is safe in terms of violent crime but is filled with thieves and scammers who target tourists. Some are aggressive—particularly with smartphone theft. Keep your phone out of sight on Métro rides and in crowded places. Wherever there are crowds (especially of tourists) there are thieves at work. It's also smart to wear a money belt. Put your wallet in your front pocket, loop your day bag over your shoulders, and keep a tight hold on your purse or shopping bag.

To replace a **passport,** you'll need to go in person to the US embassy (+33 1 43 12 22 22, 2 Avenue Gabriel, to the left as you face Hôtel Crillon, Mo: Concorde, https://fr.usembassy.gov).

If your **credit** and **debit cards** disappear, cancel and replace them, and report the loss immediately (with a mobile phone, call these 24-hour US numbers: Visa—+1 303 967 1096, MasterCard—+1 636 722 7111, and American Express—+1 336 393 1111). For more information, see RickSteves.com/help.

To claim **lost property,** contact the Bureau des Objets Trouvés (Mon-Fri 8:30-17:00, closed Sat-Sun, at police station at 36 Rue des Morillons, Mo: Convention—on south end of line 12, +33 1 53 71 53 71).

Street Smarts: When crossing the street, be careful of seemingly quiet bus/taxi/bike lanes. Parisian drivers are notorious for ignoring pedestrians. Don't assume you have the right of way, even in a cross-walk. Be mindful of cyclists as you cross, too. Cyclists ride in specially marked bike lanes on wide sidewalks and can also use lanes reserved for buses and taxis. Bikes commonly go against traffic, so always look both ways, even on one-way streets.

Around Town

Bookstores: English-language bookstores include **Shakespeare and Company** (daily 10:00-22:00, 37 Rue de la Bûcherie, across the river from Notre-Dame, Mo: St-Michel, +33 1 43 25 40 93); **Smith&Son** (Mon-Sat 9:00-19:00, Sun 12:30-19:00, near the Tuileries at 248 Rue de Rivoli, Mo: Concorde, +33 1 44 77 88 99); **Abbey Bookshop** (Mon-Sat 10:00-19:00, closed Sun, near the Cluny at 29 Rue de la Parcheminerie, Mo: Cluny La Sorbonne, +33 1 46 33 16 24); and **San Francisco Book Company** (Thu-Tue 10:00-20:00, closed Wed), north of Luxembourg Garden at 17 Rue Monsieur le Prince, Mo: Odéon, +33 1 43 29 15 70).

Laundry: Paris has no shortage of self-serve launderettes—ask your hotelier for the closest one.

WCs: Paris has some free public toilets (tipping the attendant is appropriate) and some booth-like toilets along the sidewalks. Otherwise, use restrooms in museums, or walk into any sidewalk café like you own the place, and find the toilet in the back.

Tobacco Stands (*Tabacs*): These handy little kiosks—usually just a counter inside a café—sell public-transit passes, postage stamps (though not all sell international postage), and...oh yeah, cigarettes. Just look for a *Tabac* sign and the red cylinder-shaped symbol above certain cafés. They're a slice of workaday Paris.

Charles de Gaulle Airport

Paris' main airport (code: CDG, www.charlesdegaulleairport.co.uk) has three terminals: T-1, T-2, and T-3. Most flights from the US use T-1 or T-2. Connect the three terminals on the free CDGVAL shuttle train. Allow a full hour to travel between gates across terminals T-1, T-2, and T-3. Terminals 1 and 2 have Paris Tourisme information desks, ATMs (*distributeurs*), Wi-Fi, shops, cafés, and bars. If you're returning home and want a VAT refund, look for tax-refund centers in the check-in area.

To get between Charles de Gaulle Airport and Paris, you have these options:

Taxi or Uber: Taxis charge a flat rate into Paris (€60 to the Left Bank, €55 to the Right Bank for four people with bags—beyond that, there's an extra passenger supplement). For taxi trips from Paris to the airport, have your hotel arrange it. Uber offers the same rates as taxis, but since they can't use bus-only lanes (normal taxis can), expect some added time. Charles de Gaulle does not have a designated ride-sharing pickup point, so you'll have to work out a meeting point with your driver.

RoissyBus: This bus drops you off at the Opéra Métro stop in central Paris (€15, runs 6:00-23:00, 3-4/hour, 50 minutes; buy ticket at airport Paris Tourisme desk, ticket machine, or on bus; www.ratp.fr). From there it's an easy Métro ride or €15 taxi ride to anywhere in the city.

Suburban Train: Paris' commuter RER/Train-B is the fastest public transit option to the city center (€11.50, runs 5:00-24:00, 4/hour, about 35 minutes). There are two RER-B train stations at CDG airport, a busy one at Terminal 2 and a quiet one near Terminal 3 (called Roissypole). The two stations are connected to all terminals by frequent CDGVAL shuttle trains. RER/Train-B runs directly to Gare du Nord, Châtelet-Les Halles, St. Michel, and Luxembourg; from there, you can hop the Métro. To reach RER/Train-B from any airport terminal, follow *Train* signs. (If you land at T-1, take the CDGVAL shuttle to T-3/Roissypole.)

Those Parisians

You may have heard that French people are cold and refuse to speak English. In my experience, the French are as friendly as other people (though a bit more formal) and many Parisians speak English well. But be reasonable in your expectations: French waiters are paid to be efficient, not chatty.

Parisians may appear cold when they're actually being polite and formal, respecting the fine points of culture and tradition. (From their view, those ever-smiling Americans, while friendly, are somewhat insincere.)

The best advice? Slow down. Observe the French pace of life. Impatient travelers who don't recognize the pleasures of people-watching from a sun-dappled café often misinterpret French attitudes. With *beaucoup* paid vacation and 35-hour workweeks, your hosts can't fathom why anyone would rush through their time off. By making an effort to appreciate French culture, you're likely to have a richer experience.

Other Arrival Points

Orly Airport: This easy-to-navigate airport (ORY, www.airport-orly. com) feels small, but its terminals have all the services you'd expect at a major airport: Paris Tourisme desks are in the arrivals area (a good spot to buy the Paris Museum Pass and fares for public transit into Paris). To get into Paris, you can take a taxi (€32 to Left Bank, €37 to Right Bank), Uber, or the Orlybus, which goes directly to RER/ Train-B (with access to the Luxembourg Garden area, Notre-Dame Cathedral, handy Métro line 1 at the Châtelet stop, and Gare du Nord).

Paris' Train Stations: Paris has six major stations, each serving different regions. For example, from London on the Eurostar, you'll arrive at Gare du Nord. The best all-Europe train schedule information is online at Bahn.com. The French national rail website is Sncf.

com; for online sales go to En.oui.sncf/en. Book high-speed TGV trains (also called "InOui") well in advance. To see if a rail pass could save you money, check RickSteves.com/rail.

GETTING AROUND PARIS

In Paris, you're never more than a 10-minute walk from a Métro station, and buses are everywhere. Study the fold-out Métro map at the back of this book, buy a Navigo Easy Card, learn a few handy bus lines, and Paris is yours. For more information on Paris' public transportation system, visit Ratp.fr.

Buying Tickets: The following ticket options cover transit on the Métro, public buses, and the RER/suburban train. The **Navigo Easy Card** is the easiest option for most tourists (€2, reloadable). You can add funds to your Navigo Easy card and pay as you ride (€1.90/ride), or load the card with a 10-ride pass (*"Navigo avec un carnet,"* €14.90 for Zones 1-2) or day pass (Navigo Jour, €7.50 for Zones 1-2). You can add zones to your day pass (€12.40 for Zones 1-4, covers regional destinations like Versailles). Buy your Navigo Easy or Découverte card at any staffed Métro station or at a *tabac*. All stations have machines to reload a Navigo Easy card. Or, buy a digital version on the RATP app. You'll then hold your smartphone over the card reader to enter the Métro or board a bus. For details see Ratp.fr.

By Métro

Europe's best subway system runs 5:30-1:00 in the morning, Fri-Sat until 2:00 in the morning. Find the Métro stop closest to you and the stop closest to your destination. Next, see which lines connect those two points. The lines are color-coded and numbered, and are known by their end-of-the-line stops. In the Métro station, signs direct you to the train going in your direction (e.g., *direction: La Défense*). To use your Navigo card at the Métro turnstile, touch the card to the purple pad, wait for the green validation light and the "ding," and you're on your way.

Be prepared to walk significant distances within Métro stations. To make transfers, follow *Correspondance* (Connection) signs. When you reach your destination, blue-and-white *Sortie* (exit) signs point you to the exit. Use the neighborhood maps to choose the best exit.

Métro Resources: Métro maps are in this book, free at Métro stations, online at Ratp.fr, and included on freebie Paris maps at your hotel.

Be wary of thieves in the Métro—especially while you're pre-occupied buying tickets, passing through turnstiles, and jostling to board and leave crowded trains.

By Suburban Train

The RER/suburban train works just like the Métro and uses the same ticket within the city; for outlying destinations such as Versailles, you'll need a separate, more expensive ticket. Traditionally called RER (which you'll see on signage), it's also referred to as simply "Train." These routes are indicated by thick lines on your subway map and identified by the letters A–K. Unlike the Métro, not every RER train stops at every station along the way; check the sign or screen over the platform to see if your destination is listed as a stop.

By City Bus

Bus stops are everywhere, and most come with a posted city bus map, schedule, live displays showing the next bus arrival, and a *plan du quartier* neighborhood map (there are even phone chargers at some locations). Buses use the same Navigo cards as the Métro and RER. Be sure to buy your card before boarding the bus (available at Métro stations and *tabacs*). Navigo Easy card holders can transfer from one bus to another on the same fare (within 1.5 hours), but not from bus to Métro/suburban train, or for multiple trips on the same bus line (in those cases, you'd have to buy a second fare).

Scan your Navigo card on the purple touchpad. Keep track of which stop is coming up next by following the onboard stop display. When you're ready to get off, push the red button to signal you want a stop, then exit through the central or rear door. Avoid rush hour (Mon-Fri 8:00-9:30 & 17:30-19:30), when the Métro is a better option.

Useful bus lines include bus #69, which runs east-west between the Eiffel Tower and Père Lachaise Cemetery by way of Rue Cler, Quai d'Orsay, the Louvre, Ile St. Louis, and the Marais, and scenic bus #73, which runs from the Orsay Museum up the Champs-Elysées to the Arc de Triomphe. I always check the bus stop near my hotel to see if it's convenient to my sightseeing plans.

By Uber

Uber works in Paris like it does at home, and in general works better than taxis. Drivers are nicer and more flexible than taxi drivers, although prices are roughly the same as taxis. You can generally get a car wherever you are within five minutes, and you don't have to track down a taxi stand; you can also text the driver if you don't see the car. Uber is less appealing in two instances: During rush hour, when taxis can use taxi/bus lanes while Uber drivers sit in traffic, and to get from Paris' airports to the city center (taxis have flat rates and designated pick-up areas; Uber uses dynamic pricing and you'll need to arrange a pick-up point).

By Taxi

Parisian taxis are reasonable, especially for couples and families. Fares and supplements (described in English on the rear windows) are straightforward and tightly regulated. Cabbies are required to accept four passengers, though they don't always like it. If you have more people in your group, book a larger taxi in advance.

The meter starts at €2.60 with a €7.30 minimum charge. A 20-minute ride (such as Bastille to the Eiffel Tower) costs about €25. Taxis charge higher rates at rush hour, at night, all day Sunday, and for extra passengers. To tip, round up to the next euro (at least €0.50).

You can try waving down a taxi, or find the nearest taxi stand—indicated by a circled "T" on good city maps and on many maps in this book. To order a taxi in English, call the G7 cab company (+33 1 41 27 66 99), or ask your hotelier or restaurant server to call for you; a set fee of €4 is applied for an immediate booking or €7 for reserving in advance. Taxis are tough to find during rush hour, when it's raining, on weekend nights, or on any night after the Métro closes. If you need to catch an early morning train or flight, book a taxi the day before; your hotelier can help.

By Bike

Paris is surprisingly easy by bicycle. The city is flat, and riders have access to more than 370 miles of bike lanes and many of the priority lanes for buses and taxis (be careful on these).

Neighborhood bike-path maps are available at Paris.fr/paris-respire. The TIs have a helpful "Paris à Vélo" map, which shows all dedicated bike paths. Many other versions are available for sale at newsstand kiosks, some bookstores, and department stores.

You can rent bikes from **Bike About Tours** near Hôtel de Ville (€20/day, 17 Rue du Pont Louis Philippe—see map on page 167, Mo: St-Paul, www.bikeabouttours.com) or from **Fat Tire Tours** near the Eiffel Tower (€4/hour, 24 Rue Edgar Faure, Mo: Dupleix or La Motte-Picquet-Grenelle, www.fattiretours.com/paris). Both outfits also offer good bike tours. The city's **Vélib'** program (from *vélo* + *libre* = "bike freedom") scatters thousands of bikes at racks across town for use by locals and tourists alike. This is a great option for one-way trips or rentals of a few hours or less (www.velib-metropole.fr). You can also rent a bike or electric scooter from **Lime Bikes** with its easy-to-use app (www.li.me).

MONEY

France uses the euro currency: 1 euro (€) = about $1.10. To convert prices in euros to dollars, add about 10 percent: €10 = about $11, €50 = about $55. Check www.oanda.com for the latest exchange rates. Here's my basic strategy for using money wisely in Europe.

You'll use your **credit card** for purchases both big (hotels, advance tickets) and small (little shops, food stands). A "tap-to-pay" or "contactless" card is the most widely accepted and simplest to use. Get comfortable using contactless pay options. Check to see if you already have—or can get—a tap-to-pay version of your credit card (look on the card for the tap-to-pay symbol—four curvy lines). Make sure you know the numeric, four-digit PIN for each of your cards, both debit and credit. Request it if you don't have one, as it may be required for some purchases.

Use a **debit card** at ATMs (*distributeur*) to withdraw a small amount of local cash. While most transactions are by card these days, cash can help you out of a jam if your card randomly doesn't work, and can be useful to pay for things like tips and local guides. Keep your cards and cash safe in a **money belt.**

At self-service payment machines (such as transit-ticket kiosks), US cards may not work. In this case, look for a cashier who can process your card manually—or pay in cash.

Tipping

Tipping (*donner un pourboire*) in France isn't as automatic and generous as it is in the US, but some general guidelines apply.

Restaurants: At cafés and restaurants, a 12-15 percent service charge is included in the price of what you order. It's unnecessary to tip extra, though you can for helpful service—about 5 percent. If paying with a credit card, be prepared to tip separately with cash or coins.

Taxis: For a typical ride, round up your fare a bit (for instance, if the fare is €13, pay €14).

Services: In general, if someone in the tourism or service industry does a super job for you, a small tip of a euro or two is appropriate. If you're not sure whether (or how much) to tip, ask a local for advice.

STAYING CONNECTED

Making International Calls

From a Mobile Phone: Phone numbers in this book are presented exactly as you would dial them from a US mobile phone. For international access, press and hold 0 (zero) to get a + sign, then dial the country code 33 for France) and phone number.

From a US Landline to Europe: Replace + with 011 (US/Canada access code), then dial the country code (33 for France) and phone number.

From a European Landline to the US or Europe: Replace + with 00 (Europe access code), then dial the country code (33 for France, 1 for the US) and phone number. For more phoning help, see HowToCallAbroad.com.

Using Your Phone in Europe

Sign up for an international plan. To stay connected at a lower cost, sign up for an international service plan through your carrier. Most providers offer a simple bundle that includes calling, messaging, and data.

Use free Wi-Fi whenever possible. Unless you have an unlimited-data plan, save most of your online tasks for Wi-Fi. Most accommodations in Europe offer free Wi-Fi, and many cafés offer hotspots for customers. You may also find Wi-Fi at TIs, city squares, major museums, public-transit hubs, airports, and aboard trains and buses.

Minimize use of your cellular network. Even with an international data plan, wait until you're on Wi-Fi to Skype or FaceTime, download apps, stream videos, or do other megabyte-greedy tasks. Using a navigation app such as Google Maps over a cellular network can require lots of data, so download maps when you're on Wi-Fi, then use the app offline.

Use Wi-Fi calling and messaging apps. Skype, WhatsApp, FaceTime, and Google Meet are great for making free or low-cost calls or sending texts over Wi-Fi worldwide.

RESOURCES FROM RICK STEVES

Begin your trip at RickSteves.com: This book is just one of many in my series on European travel. I also produce a public television series, *Rick Steves' Europe,* and a public radio show, *Travel with Rick Steves.* My mobile-friendly website is *the* place to explore Europe in preparation for your trip. You'll find thousands of fun articles, videos, and radio interviews; a wealth of money-saving tips; travel news dispatches; a video library of travel talks; my travel blog; our latest guidebook updates (RickSteves.com/update); and the free Rick Steves Audio Europe app with audio tours of Europe's top sights. You can also follow me on Facebook, Instagram, and Twitter.

Packing Checklist

Clothing

- ❏ 5 shirts: long- & short-sleeve
- ❏ 2 pairs pants (or skirts/capris)
- ❏ 1 pair shorts
- ❏ 5 pairs underwear & socks
- ❏ 1 pair walking shoes
- ❏ Sweater or warm layer
- ❏ Rainproof jacket with hood
- ❏ Tie, scarf, belt, and/or hat
- ❏ Swimsuit
- ❏ Sleepwear/loungewear

Money

- ❏ Debit card(s)
- ❏ Credit card(s)
- ❏ Hard cash (US $100-200)
- ❏ Money belt

Documents

- ❏ Passport
- ❏ Other required ID: vaccine card/Covid test, entry visa, etc.
- ❏ Driver's license, student ID, hostel card, etc.
- ❏ Tickets & confirmations: flights, hotels, trains, rail pass, car rental, sight entries
- ❏ Photocopies of important documents
- ❏ Insurance details
- ❏ Guidebooks & maps
- ❏ Extra passport photos
- ❏ Notepad & pen
- ❏ Journal

Toiletries

- ❏ Soap, shampoo, toothbrush, toothpaste, floss, deodorant, sunscreen, brush/comb, etc.
- ❏ Medicines & vitamins
- ❏ First-aid kit
- ❏ Glasses/contacts/sunglasses
- ❏ Face masks & hand sanitizer
- ❏ Sewing kit
- ❏ Packet of tissues (for WC)
- ❏ Earplugs

Electronics

- ❏ Mobile phone
- ❏ Camera & related gear
- ❏ Tablet/ebook reader/laptop
- ❏ Headphones/earbuds
- ❏ Chargers & batteries
- ❏ Plug adapters

Miscellaneous

- ❏ Daypack
- ❏ Sealable plastic baggies
- ❏ Laundry supplies
- ❏ Small umbrella
- ❏ Travel alarm/watch

Optional Extras

- ❏ Second pair of shoes
- ❏ Travel hairdryer
- ❏ Disinfecting wipes
- ❏ Water bottle
- ❏ Fold-up tote bag
- ❏ Small flashlight & binoculars
- ❏ Small towel or washcloth
- ❏ Tiny lock

French Survival Phrases

When using the phonetics, try to nasalize the n sound.

Good day.	Bonjour.	bohn-zhoor
Mrs. / Mr.	Madame / Monsieur	mah-dahm / muhs-yuh
Do you speak English?	Parlez-vous anglais?	par-lay-voo ahn-glay
Yes. / No.	Oui. / Non.	wee / nohn
I don't understand.	Je ne comprends pas.	
	zhuh nuh kohn-prahn pah	
Please.	S'il vous plaît.	see voo play
Thank you.	Merci.	mehr-see
I'm sorry.	Désolé.	day-zoh-lay
Excuse me.	Pardon.	par-dohn
No problem.	Pas de problème.	pah duh proh-blehm
It's good.	C'est bon.	say bohn
Goodbye.	Au revoir.	oh ruh-vwahr
one / two / three	un / deux / trois	uhn / duh / trwah
How much is it?	C'est combien?	say kohn-bee-an
I'd like / We'd like...	Je voudrais / Nous voudrions...	
	zhuh voo-dray / noo voo-dree-ohn	
...a room.	...une chambre.	ewn shahn-bruh
...a ticket to ____.	...un billet pour ____.	uhn bee-yay poor ___
Where is...?	Où est...?	oo ay
...the train station	...la gare	lah gar
...tourist information	...l'office du tourisme	loh-fees dew too-reez-muh
Where are the toilets?	Où sont les toilettes?	oo sohn lay twah-leht
men / women	hommes / dames	ohm / dahm
left / right	à gauche / à droite	ah gohsh / ah drwaht
straight	tout droit	too drwah
When does this open / close?	Ça ouvre / ferme à quelle heure?	
	sah oo-vruh / fehrm ah kehl ur	
At what time?	À quelle heure?	ah kehl ur
now / soon / later	maintenant / bientôt / plus tard	
	man-tuh-nahn / bee-an-toh / plew tar	
today / tomorrow	aujourd'hui / demain	oh-zhoor-dwee / duh-man

In a French Restaurant

I'd like / We'd like...	Je voudrais / Nous voudrions... zhuh voo-dray / noo voo-dree-ohn
...a table for one / two.	...une table pour un / deux. ewn tah-bluh poor uhn / duh
The menu (in English), please.	La carte (en anglais), s'il vous plaît. lah kart (ahn ahn-glay) see voo play
to go	à emporter ah ahn-por-tay
breakfast / lunch / dinner	petit déjeuner / déjeuner / dîner puh-tee day-zhuh-nay / day-zhuh-nay / dee-nay
special of the day	plat du jour plah dew zhoor
specialty of the house	spécialité de la maison spay-see-ah-lee-tay duh lah may-zohn
appetizers	hors d'œuvre or duh-vruh
first course (soup, salad)	entrée ahn-tray
main course (meat, fish)	plat principal plah pran-see-pahl
bread / cheese	pain / fromage pan / froh-mahzh
meat / chicken	viande / poulet vee-ahnd / poo-lay
fish / seafood	poisson / fruits de mer pwah-sohn / frwee duh mehr
mineral water	eau minérale oh mee-nay-rahl
tap water	l'eau du robinet loh dew roh-bee-nay
coffee / tea / milk	café / thé / lait kah-fay / tay / lay
wine / beer	vin / bière van / bee-ehr
red / white	rouge / blanc roozh / blahn
glass / bottle	verre / bouteille vehr / boo-tay
Cheers!	Santé! sahn-tay
The bill, please.	L'addition, s'il vous plaît. lah-dee-see-ohn see voo play
Do you accept credit cards?	Vous prenez les cartes? voo pruh-nay lay kart
tip	pourboire poor-bwahr
Delicious!	Délicieux! day-lees-yuh

For more user-friendly French phrases, check out *Rick Steves' French Phrase Book* or *Rick Steves' French, Italian & German Phrase Book*.

Start your trip at

Our website enhances this book and turns

Explore Europe

At ricksteves.com you can browse through thousands of articles, videos, photos and radio interviews, plus find a wealth of money-saving travel tips for planning your dream trip. And with our mobile-friendly website, you can easily access all this great travel information anywhere you go.

TV Shows

Preview the places you'll visit by watching entire half-hour episodes of *Rick Steves' Europe* (choose from all 100 shows) on-demand, for free.

ricksteves.com

your travel dreams into affordable reality

Radio Interviews

Enjoy ready access to Rick's vast library of radio interviews covering travel tips and cultural insights that relate specifically to your Europe travel plans.

Travel Forums

Learn, ask, share! Our online community of savvy travelers is a great resource for first-time travelers to Europe, as well as seasoned pros.

Travel News

Subscribe to our free Travel News e-newsletter, and get monthly updates from Rick on what's happening in Europe.

Classroom Europe®

Check out our free resource for educators with 500 short video clips from the *Rick Steves' Europe* TV show.

Audio Europe™

Rick's Free Travel App

Get your FREE Rick Steves Audio Europe™ app to enjoy...

- Dozens of self-guided tours of Europe's top museums, sights and historic walks
- Hundreds of tracks filled with cultural insights and sightseeing tips from Rick's radio interviews
- All organized into handy geographic playlists
- For Apple and Android

With Rick whispering in your ear, Europe gets even better.

Find out more at ricksteves.com

Pack Light and Right

Gear up for your next adventure at ricksteves.com

Light Luggage

Pack light and right with Rick Steves' affordable, custom-designed rolling carry-on bags, backpacks, day packs and shoulder bags.

Accessories

From packing cubes to moneybelts and beyond, Rick has personally selected the travel goodies that will help your trip go smoother.

Shop at ricksteves.com

Rick Steves has

Experience maximum Europe

Save time and energy

This guidebook is your independent-travel toolkit. But for all it delivers, it's still up to you to devote the time and energy it takes to manage the preparation and logistics that are essential for a happy trip. If that's a hassle, there's a solution.

Rick Steves Tours

A Rick Steves tour takes you to Europe's most interesting places with great guides and small groups.

great tours, too!

with minimum stress

We follow Rick's favorite itineraries, ride in comfy buses, stay in family-run hotels, and bring you intimately close to the Europe you've traveled so far to see. Most importantly, we take away the logistical headaches so you can focus on the fun.

Join the fun

This year we'll take thousands of free-spirited travelers—nearly half of them repeat customers—along with us on four dozen different itineraries, from Ireland to Italy to Athens. Is a Rick Steves tour the right fit for your travel dreams? Find out at ricksteves.com, where you can check seat availability and sign up.

Europe is best experienced with happy travel partners. We hope you can join us.

See our itineraries at ricksteves.com

A Guide for Every Trip

BEST OF GUIDES
Full-color guides in an easy-to-scan format, focusing on top sights and experiences in popular destinations

COMPREHENSIVE GUIDES
City, country, and regional guides printed on Bible-thin paper. Packed with detailed coverage for a multi-week trip exploring iconic sights and more

Many guides are available as ebooks.

POCKET GUIDES
Compact guides for shorter city trips

Amsterdam	Italy's Cinque Terre	Prague
Athens	London	Rome
Barcelona	Munich & Salzburg	Venice
Florence	Paris	Vienna

SNAPSHOT GUIDES
Focused single-destination coverage

Basque Country: Spain & France
Copenhagen & the Best of Denmark
Dublin
Dubrovnik
Edinburgh
Hill Towns of Central Italy
Krakow, Warsaw & Gdansk
Lisbon
Loire Valley
Madrid & Toledo
Milan & the Italian Lakes District
Naples & the Amalfi Coast
Nice & the French Riviera
Normandy
Northern Ireland
Norway
Reykjavík
Rothenburg & the Rhine
Sevilla, Granada & Southern Spain
St. Petersburg, Helsinki & Tallinn
Stockholm

CRUISE PORTS GUIDES
Reference for cruise ports of call

Mediterranean Cruise Ports
Scandinavian & Northern European
   Cruise Ports

TRAVEL SKILLS & CULTURE
Greater information and insight

Europe 101
Europe Through the Back Door
Europe's Top 100 Masterpieces
European Christmas
European Easter
European Festivals
For the Love of Europe
Italy for Food Lovers
Travel as a Political Act

PHRASE BOOKS & DICTIONARIES

French
French, Italian & German
German
Italian
Portuguese
Spanish

PLANNING MAPS

Britain, Ireland & London
Europe
France & Paris
Germany, Austria & Switzerland
Iceland
Ireland
Italy
Scotland
Spain & Portugal

PHOTO CREDITS

Avalon Travel
Hachette Book Group
1700 Fourth Street
Berkeley, CA 94710

Printed in Thailand for Imago
Fifth Edition
First printing July 2023

ISBN 978-1-64171-416-7

For the latest on Rick's lectures, guidebooks, tours, public radio show, and public television series, contact Rick Steves' Europe, 130 Fourth Avenue North, Edmonds, WA 98020, +1 425 771 8303, RickSteves.com, rick@ricksteves.com.

Rick Steves' Europe
Managing Editor: Jennifer Madison Davis
Assistant Managing Editor: Cathy Lu
Editors: Glenn Eriksen, Tom Griffin, Suzanne Kotz, Rosie Leutzinger, Teresa Nemeth, Jessica Shaw, Carrie Shepherd
Editorial & Production Assistant: Megan Simms
Graphic Content Director: Sandra Hundacker
Maps & Graphics: Orin Dubrow, David C. Hoerlein, Lauren Mills, Mary Rostad, Laura Terrenzio

Avalon Travel
Senior Editor and Series Manager: Madhu Prasher
Associate Managing Editor: Jamie Andrade
Editors: Sierra Machado, Rachael Sablik
Copy Editor: Kelly Lydick
Proofreader: Maggie Ryan
Indexer: Claire Splan
Production & Typesetting: Rue Flaherty
Cover Design: Kimberly Glyder Design
Interior Design: Darren Alessi
Maps & Graphics: Kat Bennett, John Culp

Let's Keep on Travelin'

Your trip doesn't need to end.

Follow Rick on social media!